Handbook
of
CHRISTIAN
PUPPETRY

Grace Harp

ILLUSTRATED BY
Jan Barnes

ACCENT PUBLICATIONS
Denver, Colorado

About the Author . . .

Grace Harp is well-qualified to write on the subject of Christian puppetry. She holds degrees from San Francisco State College and Biola University, and has done graduate work at Los Angeles State and Fuller Seminary.

Her teaching experience includes both public and Christian schools, as well as instructing in the Christian Education Department at Biola. Mrs. Harp is well-known for her puppet workshops in Sunday School conventions in California. She has also conducted workshops for the Association of Christian Schools Interntional, Puppeteers of America, and the Fellowship of Christian Puppeteers.

She makes her home in Los Gatos, California.

Accent Publications
12100 West Sixth Avenue
P.O. Box 15337
Denver, Colorado 80215

Library of Congress Catalog Number 84-70000

ISBN 0-89636-125-X
Fourth Printing

CONTENTS

1

Meet "Friend" Puppets and "Story" Puppets

In all aspects of Christian education the use of puppets can create a warm at-home atmosphere for the purpose of treating spiritual truth with importance and dignity while emphasizing the reality, power and goodness of God. Used properly, they will contribute greatly to the learning of accurate Christian concepts.

As Christian workers, however, we should recognize certain limitations when an object of fantasy, such as a puppet, is used to teach Christian truths. I believe, for example, that a "friend" puppet—as a puppet—should never be a Christian. (If "friend" puppets are presented as Christians, it must follow that Jesus died for puppets and that puppet Christians will go to heaven with people Christians. We would not want to confuse even one child's mind with such a misconception.)

On the other hand, it would be possible for a "story" puppet to assume the name and identity of a Christian person in a dramatization without problem. Then it would not be the puppet itself who was a Christian, but rather, the real person he is representing who has the relationship with God.

Before considering the scope of puppetry in Christian education and giving how-to-do-it instructions, I have listed certain guidelines which I have found to be important in my puppet ministry.

GUIDELINES FOR PUPPETRY IN CHRISTIAN EDUCATION

1. A puppet in the role of itself should never be a Christian.
2. Distinguish between kinds of puppets—*friend* puppets and *story* puppets.
3. *Friend* puppets interact with people and they never pretend to be capable of a relationship with God.
4. *Story* puppets take the parts of people in dramatizations, including Christians who have a relationship with God.
5. An animal puppet should not represent a person in a Christian story dramatization.
6. We should avoid using a puppet to represent Jesus.
7. Christian stories and conversations must be believable.
8. Language and behavior of puppets should usually be commendable.
9. We should adapt ideas and scripts to the needs of different age groups and keep variety in the use of puppets.
10. It is good practice to involve children in puppetry whenever that is practical.

To avoid the pitfalls of having an object of fantasy, such as a puppet, pretend to be a Christian in its talk and actions (guideline 1), we find the solution in following the second guideline, that of distinguishing between the kinds of puppets. To do this, divide the puppets you use into two categories—*friend* puppets and *story* puppets.

Friend puppets are those that recognize the presence of people. They appear in combination with a person, or interact with a group of children. They are presented as just what they are—puppets.

Story puppets, as the name implies, take the parts of people in stories. They assume the names and identities of the characters they portray in dramatizations. They can be used to dramatize isolated incidents, partial stories, or complete stories. Thus, they may act and speak like Christians in the scripts.

Let us get better acquainted with these two kinds of puppets.

Friend Puppets

Puppets to use for friend puppets. A friend puppet can be any type of puppet—animal, person, or monster-type puppet. If you are starting a puppet ministry with just one friend puppet, an animal puppet is a good choice, as children usually enjoy animal puppets more than people puppets, and small children may be afraid of monster puppets.

It is an advantage (though not at all necessary) to have more than one friend puppet. Additional puppets add variety to a puppet ministry, and also make it possible for puppets to talk to each other as well as to people. A family of friend puppets can consist of a mixture of any type and variety of puppets.

Names for friend puppets. Children love names and it would be wise to give your friend puppets names. It is best to use names that are not common; a child who has the same name as a puppet my feel ill-at-ease. If you wish to invent a name, change one or more vowels in a word (any word), switch the position of the syllables in a word, or take one or more syllables from two or three words and combine them to make a new word, such as Rufford, or Shepley. Some names may be made up from an activity or a characteristic, such as Hummer, Happy, or Yelper. Sometimes you can just choose a crazy-sounding word for a name, like Roquefort and Pistachio, and the children love such names.

Children may want to give a puppet the same name as a puppet they know from television. This is neither proper nor desirable. If children want to call a frog puppet, Kermit, have the puppet say: "My name is Farley. Kermit is a frog and I'm a frog, but my name is Farley—Farley Frog."

Friend puppets are neutral. Friend puppets are neither Christian nor non-Christian. They are limited to being themselves. They are not actors playing the part of another personality. They are just puppets interacting with people. Friend puppets do not assume that God had them in mind when He created the universe or authored the Bible. They are observers of God's dealing with people. We should not ask children to believe that a friend puppet represents a person with an eternal soul because the difference between the puppet and the real people he is interactng with is much too obvious.

Friend puppets do not: (1) talk about their love for God or God's love for them; (2) speak of trying to please God; nor (3) pray, lead a group in prayer or ask people to pray for them.

Friend puppets are *never sad* because they are puppets and are not capable of a personal relationship with God.

Instead, friend puppets are *excited, delighted,* and *overjoyed* that they can be used to help children learn about God and the relationship that people can have with Him.

If a child asks a friend puppet if he is a Christian, have a puppet cheerfully reply: "That's a question for a person and I'm a puppet. Let me ask the person working me... Say, Mrs. Jones, are you a Christian?... Sure enough, she is. Isn't that great?" Any question involving a relationship with God can be handled similarly. Children think of a puppet as a personality separate from the puppeteer, so a puppet should not speak as if he were the puppeteer, capable of a relationship with God.

WHAT FRIEND PUPPETS DO AND SAY.

1) *Welcome chidren; make children feel wanted and loved; take attendance.*

2) *Engage in fun-type conversation with a person or another puppet.*

3) *Introduce the theme of the day, the next song, names of story characters, etc.*

4) *Make announcements.*

5) *Acknowledge and appreciate God's provisions for people and animals.* Friend puppets say: "Isn't it nice to have sunshine, rain, day and night? God makes them all and gives them to every person and every animal in the whole world."

6) *Acknowledge and appreciate God's realtionship with people.* Friend puppets say: "God sent Jesus to die for every person in the world. Isn't it wonderful that God loved people that much? Do you know that any time you boys and girls want to talk to God, you can? You don't have to wake Him up first, or be in a certain place or anything like that. And God answers prayer."

Friend puppets do not say: "God sent Jesus to die for *me*." Or "*I* can pray and God will answer."

7) *Encourage boys and girls to accept Jesus as their Savior and live the Bible way.* Friend puppets say: "I hope all you boys and girls love Jesus and are living for Him." "Boys and girls, you should thank God each day for everything you have." "Would God be pleased if you did something extra to help at home this week?" "I know a boy who is a Christian and he has a problem. . . What do you think he should do?"

Friend puppets do not say: "*I* want to live for God." "*I* thank God for. . ." "I will do something so *I* can please God." "*I'm* a Christian and have a problem. . . ."

8) *Teach and learn Bible verses, Bible stories and related material.* Friend puppets are enthusiastic teachers and learners of the Bible and related material. They enjoy teaching other puppets and children. And they enjoy being taught by other puppets, children and adult leaders.

Friend puppets do not apply Bible truths to themselves; only to people.

NOTE: *Friend puppets and the Bible.* Friend puppets do not think that the Bible is God's message to them. However, they do ask for (or happen to remember) a Bible verse or Bible-based advice. When they apply this information in their puppet world and it works, they proclaim: "The Bible way is the best way" and "You boys and girls should live your whole lives the way the Bible says you should live."

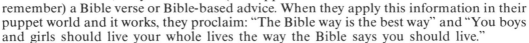

9) *Teach and learn songs; listen to children sing; ask children to sing a certain song; sing with children; sing special numbers.* Puppet songs (songs appropriate for friend puppets to sing) are songs that declare truth, but do not involve a personal relationship with God on the part of the singer. Puppet songs are such as: "Jesus Loves the Little Children of the World" and "God Can Do Everything." Friend puppets enjoy listening, and perhaps keep time, as children sing people songs such as: "Jesus Loves Me" and "Oh, How I Love My Lord."

For a special number (when a puppet sings by himself), certain people songs can be changed into puppet songs by changing one or more words. "Jesus Loves Me" can be changed to "Jesus Loves You." "I Have Decided to Follow Jesus" can be sung as a question: "Have you decided to follow Jesus?. . . . Should no one join you, will you still follow?" In some cases, extra words and a slight revision of the tune are necessary.

The only time a puppet should sing a people song is in a Christian-story dramatization. In this case, the puppet would be singing to another story character—not to the audience.

10) *Be a teacher's helper.* Friend puppets make announcements; tell teacher the names of those present; welcome visitors; tell part of a story; hand out awards; ask review questions, etc.

11) *Participate in classroom activities.* Friend puppets can earn points in contests, bring food for needy families, and even participate in a special offering—such as an offering

that will be used to buy Christmas presents for children of missionary families.

Friend puppets participate just to join in or so that people will be happy—not so they can please God.

12) *Demonstrate a change in behavior—from bad to good.* Demonstrations of poor behavior and the change to good behavior occur during the normal course of events—like when one puppet is accidently knocked down and doesn't care to forgive the one at fault, or when two puppets want to give the same announcement or when a puppet doesn't want to tell where he hid the flannelgraph figures for the Bible story. Behavior incidents deal with forgiveness, sharing, pride, grumbling, selfishness, stubbornness, etc. *Friend* puppets, in regard to themselves and a change in their behavior, do not mention salvation, prayer, trusting God or anything else that involves a personal relationship with God.

NOTE: How to arrange for a change in behavior. A change in behavior can come about in several ways: (1) The misbehaving puppet simply corrects his behavior—he might express his thoughts out loud, asking questions and answering them, convincing himself to change; (2) one of the puppets involved suggests a solution which the other puppet agrees to; or (3) if there are two puppets on stage, the one not at fault exits momentarily and the one at fault asks the audience for information or advice. If children give poor advice, the puppet disregards it and decides to do what he now thinks to be right.

SAMPLE SCRIPT—Involving a change in behavior from bad to good.
(Two puppets have been asked to make an announcement together. As they enter the stage #1 accidently bumps into #2, knocking him down.)
#1:   Oops, sorry. I wasn't looking.
#2:   (DISGUSTEDLY AS HE GETS UP) "Sorry. . . sorry!" Just look what you've done. My clothes are dirty and my elbow lost a whole layer of skin!
#1:   I really am sorry. I didn't mean to bump into you. Please forgive me.
#2:   Forgive you? I'll have to think about that. Come back after a while. (#1 EXITS, #2 SPEAKS TO AUDIENCE) That fellow wants me to forgive him and I don't want to. Does the Bible say anything about forgiving others?. . . Do you think I should forgive him? (Not "Do you think God wants me to forgive him?"). . . O.K., I'll try out that forgiving idea in my puppet world. (#1 ENTERS) Oh, hello! I sure acted dumb after you bumped into me. I forgive you. Can we be friends?
#1:   Sure.
#2:   (TO AUDIENCE) The words God has given to people in the Bible sure are wonderful words. The Bible way is the best way. I hope all you boys and girls live your lives the way the Bible says to live. And now my friend and I will make an announcement together. I feel so good I might even sing my part!

NOTE: How to handle a "grouch-type" puppet. The grouch on the Sesame Street television show has a warped view of society. His taste is for "garbage" and he is generally unpleasant and uncooperative. It is important to note that the Grouch is not intentionally obnoxious—he just doesn't know how to be nice. When he is told how to get along with others he sometimes falls into line, but he does so reluctantly because this "rubs him the wrong way." The Grouch's undesirable attitudes and behavior are exaggerated to the extent that children will, hopefully, realize that they don't want these traits to dominate their lives.

The other puppets and the people on Sesame Street do not condone nor make light of the Grouch's ideas and activities. Neither do they retaliate in kind. Rather, they often try to talk him out of his contrary attitudes and behavior by pointing out a better way.

On occasion, the Grouch expresses his liking for pickle ice cream, bad weather, etc. and, with good intentions, gives something like an ugly withered plant for a present. These odd tastes are not a behavior issue but, as most children reject these ideas, this may help them to also reject the Grouch's negative behavior.

If you use a grouch-type puppet (perhaps with the name, "Vinegar"), be sure that the end result isn't that children think it is funny, smart, or the "in-thing" to think and act like the puppet. Through a series of discussion questions it could be brought out that we people are sometimes grouchy because something inside is bothering us. When we ask Jesus to forgive us and enable us to think rightly, then we can be happy again and not be a grouch. (If the discussion involves a puppet, take care that asking Jesus' forgiveness applies only to people—not to puppets.)

If you have a grouch-type puppet that gradually changes to a pleasant character—because of encouragement to live and think right—and you wish to continue "grouch-lessons," introduce another grouch. The original grouch could either move away or remain on the scene.

As one puppeteer said, "Children identify with grouchiness. When grouchiness is corrected, they realize there's hope for them."

In the interest of realism, some Christian educators feel it is better not to have a separate grouch-type puppet. They believe the concept is better taught if a regular puppet is grouchy on occasion, with the reason for grouchiness given and the overcoming of grouchiness demonstrated.

NOTE: If you choose, on occasion, not to follow the guidelines for friend puppets—and you present a friend puppet as capable of a relationship with God—be sure that any young children in the audience understand that the puppet is, for this occasion, pretending to be a real person.

Story Puppets

Puppets to use for story puppets. It is a good idea, but not necessary (except for preschoolers) to have a separate set of Christian story puppets. Friend people puppets can become Christian story puppets. But in order for friend puppets to step out of their neutrality, the teacher, a narrator puppet, or the puppets involved should make it clear to children that the puppets are pretending to be real people and that what happens in the dramatization is not happening to the puppets, but rather to the people they represent. Make this explanation in such a way that children won't feel you are insulting their intelligence. The amount and type of explanation will depend on the ages of the children.

Names for story puppets. A puppet used in a story has no name for itself. It takes on the name of the character it is playing in the story.

Puppet playing the part of Jesus. You may hold a different opinion, but I do not recommend that a puppet be used to represent Jesus. Children are forming concepts of Jesus, and representing the Son of God with an animated puppet is a serious matter, it seems to me. It is different from using a picture of Jesus. A picture doesn't talk or move, and when using a picture or a flannelgraph figure of Jesus, it doesn't seem to "come alive" in the way a puppet does.

Dramatizing stories about Jesus with puppets can be performed in the following ways without a Jesus puppet. (The scenes should be kept short.)

1) Puppets act out as much of the story as possible, but before a scene that involves Jesus, all puppets exit the stage and the scene with Jesus is done with voices only. To help identify who is speaking and what is happening, story characters mention another's name when speaking to that person. On occasion, story characters might voice their thoughts out loud to themselves. The voice for Jesus should sound normal—not affected or of odd quality.

2) Puppets exit (or remain on stage in a "frozen" position with backs to audience) while a narrator (either a narrator puppet, person outside stage, or off-stage voice of a puppeteer) tells the part of the story involving Jesus. Narration can be the quotation

of Scripture, your own words, or a combination of the two.

3) Puppets exit, pause for a count of five, reenter and talk about what happened when Jesus was present.

4) Puppets look off to the side, or behind them, and comment on what they pretend to see happening and/or repeat what they pretend to hear being said: Why are those two blind men bothering Jesus?. . . Jesus is asking them if they think He can heal them. . . . They think He can. . . . Jesus is touching their eyes. . . . They can see! Then one or both former blind men could pass by and tell the onlookers about their healing.

5) Instead of using regular-type puppets, use flannelgraph figures (including Jesus) taped to holders (plastic drinking straws, rulers, pencils). Or instead of flannelgraph figures, cut out silhouettes. If two identical profile silhouettes are taped or glued together—with a holder between them—the figure can be turned to face either direction.

In Summary

FRIEND PUPPETS. In the first illustration above, the horizontal communication arrows are intended to visualize the thought that friend puppets communicate on a horizontal level—with people and other puppets. There is no vertical arrow because friend puppets do not communicate up—with God.

Friend puppets declare, learn and teach about God, and test Bible information, but all in a NEUTRAL framework.

NEUTRAL-STORY DRAMATIZATIONS. No character in a neutral-story dramatization has a personal relationship with God. Therefore there is no vertical communication arrow in the second illustration. Neutral-story dramatizations NEED NOT BE BELIEVABLE unless the story is true and/or respect is due the characters.

CHRISTIAN-STORY DRAMATIZATIONS. As the vertical arrow indicates in the third illustration, involving story puppets, at least one character in a Christian-story dramatization has a personal relationship with God. Therefore Christian-story dramatizations should be BELIEVABLE in all possible respects.

(See later chapters for more information about neutral-story and Christian-story dramatizations.)

2

Puppets in Action

One puppet is all you need to begin your ministry with puppets. As you progress, you will probably want to add more to your collection. It is a good idea to have a variety of puppets, and there is no reason why you cannot have different types of puppets in the same performance. Movable-mouth puppets, like on Sesame Street, can hold attention longer when speaking, but glove puppets are also effective and they have the advantage of being able to move their arms and handle props.

If you wish to purchase movable-mouth puppets or other types of ready-made puppets, or patterns and directions for making several types of puppets, see the Resource List at the back of the book for suppliers of these items.

Making Puppets

The directions given here can be used for making a glove puppet, a rod puppet, or a puppet that has a head separate from the body.

MATERIALS

Head:
A double sheet of newspaper and tape. Or 3" or 4" styrofoam ball. (With a newspaper head, cotton or Dacron pillow stuffing to smooth the circle is recommended but optional.)

To secure neck and hands:
3 rubber bands or vegetable twists (or 1 rubber band or vegetable twist and 2 plastic or metal rings that fit over tip of your thumb).

Head covering and costume:
Square or rectangle of any fairly soft non-see-through material at least 14" wide and as long as desired. Color can be skin tones or blue, green, etc. All-purpose cloths such as Handi-Wipes (grocery store item), can be used even though they have a design.

Headdress for Bible characters:
Plain or striped cloth.

Hair:
Yarn, fake-fur cloth, chenille pom-poms (yardage store item), felt or non-ravel material, including all-purpose cloths.

Eyes:
Black and white felt, cardboard or art paper (pink, blue, etc., can be used instead of white). Or purchase plastic wiggle eyes (craft store item) 3/4" in diameter (23mm) or larger size recommended.

Nose:
Small circle of felt, colored paper, non-ravel cloth or covered button. To make ball-type nose you will need circle of material, needle and thread, and stuffing (small styrofoam ball or pillow stuffing).

Mouth:
Felt, non-ravel cloth, paper or colored tape.

Ears:
Same material as head covering and stuffing, or chenille pom-poms.

White craft glue, straight pins, lightweight cardboard, tape:
These items are not needed for all puppets; check directions below.

PROCEDURE

1. *Prepare Head.* (Make either A or B head.)

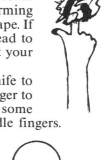

A. Newspaper head. Crumple up a sheet of newspaper (do not tear sheet in half). Insert your index finger halfway into head and continue forming newspaper into a ball shape around your finger. Secure newspaper with tape. If desired, wrap thin layer of cotton or Dacron pillow stuffing around head to give a smoother look. (For larger head, use more newspaper and insert your three middle fingers.)

B. Styrofoam ball head. Use an apple corer or handle of a table knife to gouge out a finger hole. Make hole deep enough to admit your index finger to the first joint (deepen hole later if desired; if hole becomes too deep, push some stuffing back into hole). For 4" ball, make hole to fit your three middle fingers.

2. *Add Head Covering and Costume.* One piece of material covers the head and becomes the basic costume as well. With your finger(s) in puppet's head, place center of material over top of head. Gather material around puppet's neck, gathering more to the back of the head than to the front. Place a rubber band or vegetable twist loosely around puppet's neck.

3. *Form Arms and Hands.* This is optional, but if you wish the puppet to have arms and hands, put your index finger in puppet's head and spread out your thumb and middle finger; or with your three middle fingers in the head, spread out your thumb and little finger. Gather material around the puppet's "arms" and place rubber band, vegetable twist or plastic cafe curtain ring over tips of thumb and finger.

NOTE: For a quick change of puppets or to make it easier for a child to hold a puppet, insert a dowel or cardboard tube from pants hanger into head of puppet as shown at right. This type of puppet is known as a rod puppet.

4. *Add Hair. Removable wig:* Attach hair to a skullcap—cloth shaped like top of puppet's head. *Yarn hair:* Tie strands or loops of yarn together in the middle. Or sew strands or loops to strip of felt or non-ravel cloth. *Bangs:* Cut yarn short in front or add extra yarn. *Layered hair:* Sew one end of strands or loops to strip of cloth. Attach to head one above the other. *Pom-pom hair:* Glue pom-poms close together all over head. *Fake-fur hair:* Experiment with different shapes.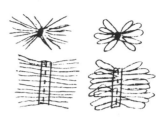

For a girl you can use a long rectangular strip and tie it tight one-third the way in from each end. *Felt or cloth hair:* Cut felt, non-ravel cloth or all-purpose cloth in a circle. Lightly mark the crown either at the center or off-center. (It's a good idea to experiment  with newspaper hair first.) Cut as shown by broken lines. If ends of strands are too wide, you might want to cut them up a ways from the outer edge. And/or try two layers of hair. 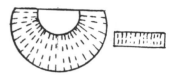 Another style is to fold a circle in half before or after cutting and place on head in a folded position. To make bangs for this style of hairpiece, cut a small rectangular piece of material and slit one side almost to the edge. Place bangs under hairpiece to hide raw edge of bangs. Pin hairpiece or wig to puppet. Beard: Make of yarn or fur and pin on.

5. *Headdress.* For Bible characters you will want to make a headdress. You may need no hair in this case, or perhaps only a puff of hair in front. For male character, make headdress of rectangular piece of cloth. If stiff material is used, fold sides toward back of head and fold top down. Sew to secure folds. For female character, use a half-circle of soft cloth or a whole circle folded in half. Or use the larger portion of an oval-shaped piece of soft coth. Pin headdress to puppet.

6. *Add Eyes.* To make eyes of cardboard, colored paper or felt: Hold a dime, or slightly smaller button, on a small square of black and cut around dime or button. Cut around a nickle on white or other color. Glue circles together and glue to head midway between top and bottom of head. The position of eyes is very important. The tendency is to place eyes too far up on the head.

eyes too high

If you are using plastic wiggle eyes and the eyes have a plastic (not paper) backing, and your glue does not hold them securely to puppet, coat the back of the eyes with contact cement (variety or hardware store). Let the cement dry overnight. Then most any glue will hold them secure.

eyes centered

For removable (pin-on) eyes, cut thin cardboard smaller than the eyes. Push a straight pin through the center of the cardboard. Glue cardboard to back of eyes as shown at right. Or, instead of cardboard, you can push a straight pin through the sticky side of a piece of sturdy tape (or 8 layers of transparent tape) and press tape to eye.

7. *Add Nose.* Pom-poms make good noses. Or cut circle or partial circle of paper, cloth, or felt. Or, cut circle of cloth about 1¼" in diameter. Sew gathering stitch near edge. Stuff with cotton, Dacron or small styrofoam ball. Pull thread tight and secure. Glue or pin nose to puppet same as eyes. Nose can be quite close to eyes.

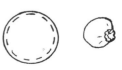

8. *Add Mouth.* The expression of a puppet should not be extra happy or extra sad unless the puppet is always like that. However, the mouth should have a slight curve. Experiment with different shapes and sizes. Pin or glue on mouth. Mouth can be quite close to nose.

9. *Add Ears* (optional). Cut half circles of material used for head covering. Sew together, turn and stuff. Glue or pin to puppet at eye level. Or use pom-poms for ears.

VARIATIONS

Rod puppet: Form newspaper head over rod, or push rod into styrofoam ball. Hold onto rod and spread your thumb and index finger to make arms of puppet.

Alternate coverings for styrofoam ball head. You can use craft waterbase spray paint to cover a styrofoam head. Or you can cover a ball with felt or stretchy material such as knit cloth, socks or nylon hose (two layers of hosiery may be required). To make felt covering: wet felt, place center on face of puppet and pull hard around ball. There should be no wrinkles on front half of ball. In back, pinch wrinkles so they stand up and secure them in standing position with straight pins. When felt is dry, trim wrinkles with scissors. Spread glue on styrofoam in wrinkle areas so cut edges of felt will stay flat against styrofoam. There need be no felt where hair will cover styrofoam.

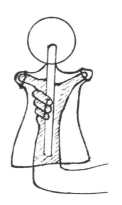

Making Costumes

When making costumes for your puppets it is wise to experiment with scrap material to determine the size you need. These patterns are designed for a costume which has either the puppeteer's finger(s) or a rod inserted into the neck and then into the puppet's head.

Costume for puppet with separate head covering. With a piece of cloth over your index finger or three middle fingers, insert your finger(s) into puppet's head. Or cut a costume as shown at right (see Costume/Patterns). The costume will cover your index finger or your three middle fingers, as well as your spread-out thumb and finger.

Longer neck for puppet. Roll a 3" wide strip of lightweight cardboard (index card, file folder, etc.) three or more times around your index finger or three middle fingers, with bottom of cardboard resting at the second finger joint. Secure cardboard tube with tape. Glue tube into finger hole in puppet's head, leaving about 1-1/2" protruding. Cover protruding part with same material as head covering and glue in place, with seam at back of neck.

If you wish to hang a costume on the neck: glue a piece of rope around the bottom of the cardboard tube. Or instead of rope, glue string around bottom of tube until it is about 1/4" thick. Or instead of rope or string sew Vellux to the bottom of the cardboard tube and also to the neck of each costume. For permanent costume, use rope and sew neck of costume to rope.

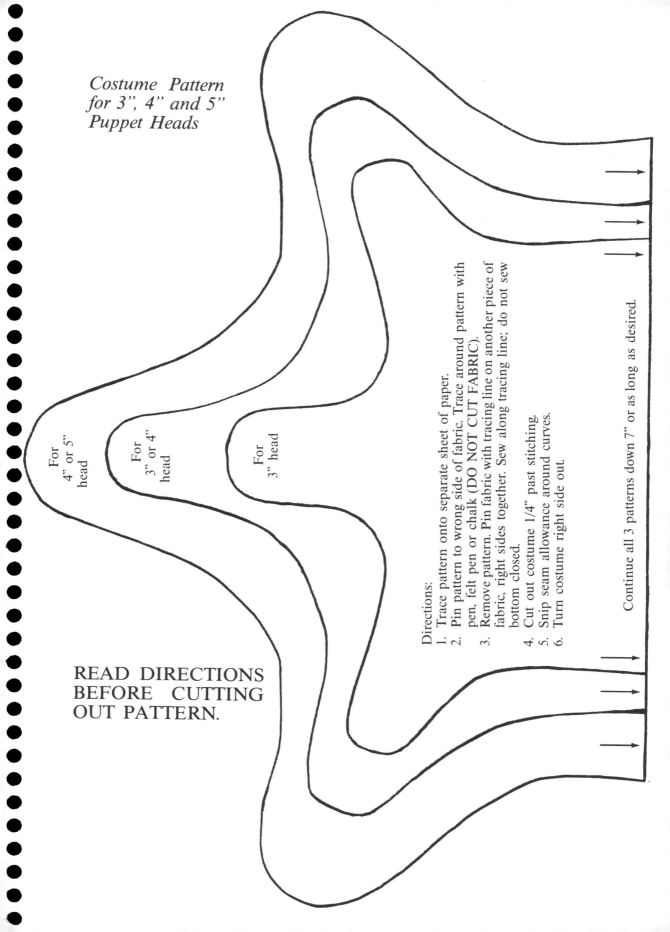

Costume Pattern for 3", 4" and 5" Puppet Heads

READ DIRECTIONS BEFORE CUTTING OUT PATTERN.

For 4" or 5" head

For 3" or 4" head

For 3" head

Directions:
1. Trace pattern onto separate sheet of paper.
2. Pin pattern to wrong side of fabric. Trace around pattern with pen, felt pen or chalk (DO NOT CUT FABRIC).
3. Remove pattern. Pin fabric with tracing line on another piece of fabric, right sides together. Sew along tracing line; do not sew bottom closed.
4. Cut out costume 1/4" past stitching.
5. Snip seam allowance around curves.
6. Turn costume right side out.

Continue all 3 patterns down 7" or as long as desired.

Basic Pattern for 4" and 5" Puppet Heads and Overgarments

For neck that encloses puppeteer's fingers, extend pattern straight up 2".

READ DIRECTIONS BEFORE CUTTING PATTERN OUT OF FABRIC.

Permission given to original purchaser to photocopy pattern for personal or church use.

Neck of costume can be gathered and glued to a rod that will be inserted into puppet's head. Or if neck of costume is extended and sewed closed, puppeteer's fingers can be inserted into neck of costume and then into puppet's head.

PLACE ON FOLD OF MATERIAL

EXTEND PATTERN DOWN 4"
OR AS LONG AS DESIRED

Directions:

1. Trace pattern onto another piece of paper before cutting it out along line.
2. For front, pin pattern to wrong side of fabric. Trace around pattern with pen, felt pen or chalk. Cut along tracing line. For a larger costume, cut 1/4" or 1/2" past tracing line.
3. For back (which should be wider), pin pattern on fold of wrong side of fabric, placing pattern 1-1/2" away from fold. Trace around pattern and cut out along line.
4. With right sides together, pin or baste pieces together. Sew, using 3/16" seam allowance. Do not sew bottom closed. Sew neck closed only if neck will enclose puppeteer's fingers.
5. Snip seam allowance around curves.
6. Turn costume right side out. If needed, sew dart in back of neck or gather neck to desired size.

Overgarments: If you wish to make a dress, shirt and pants, or a coat, cut them 1/4" larger than original costume. To make shirt and pants, cut the pattern in two at the waist and add 3/16" seam allowance between the two pieces. Sew shirt to pants.

To make what appear to be pants, cut a narrow triangular-shaped section from front of skirt and glue along the inside edges a larger triangular piece of contrasting color felt. (Use dots of glue, as a strip of glue dries stiff.) A "fly" for pants can be embroidered on with contrasting color thread. Cut sleeve of coat or shirt straight across the end (instead of the curve) and do not sew closed. Design hands and sew inside wrists, if desired.

Stages for Puppets

STAGES FOR A PUPPET (but not for the puppeteer)

To provide a stage for a puppet all you need to do is hold a piece of cardboard or folded grocery bag in your hand and manipulate the puppet behind it. Or you can position the puppet over a flannelboard or piano. A large piece of cardboard or wood paneling leaning against a table and held in place by chairs can also be used for a stage. You can make a stage by cutting two panels from a cardboard box and taping them together. The stage can rest on a table or on the floor—depending on the size.

Stages you make will be more attractive if you border them with 1-1/2" or 2" wide tape; and you might want to cover the stage with paper or cloth of a solid color before applying the tape.

YOU DON'T NEED TO BE A VENTRILOQUIST TO USE A PUPPET WHEN YOU ARE IN VIEW OF AN AUDIENCE. If you can remember to look at the puppet when you are speaking for him or her, you will find that the average person will not care, or even notice that your lips are moving. If someone does happen to bring up the subject, you can reply, "Yes, I know, but isn't it fun to use puppets this way?"

To keep yourself out of sight you can kneel or sit behind a piano, an overturned table or a flannelboard that has a sheet draped over it. Or cut and tape together two or more sections of cardboard that are large enough to conceal you. A dressmaker's cutting board can be a stage. They are usually available at a reasonable cost. If the six panels of the cutting board do not stay in the desired position, cut the panels apart and tape them back together so each panel stays 1/2" apart from the adjacent panel. Cover the exposed tape with another piece of tape so the tape will not stick to itself when the stage is folded.

ENCLOSED STAGE WITH ONE-WAY VIEWING SCREEN
(Stage folds flat for storage.)

A stage with a one-way viewing screen gives you the advantage of being able to see the puppets and the audience yet remain hidden from view. The puppeteer can see the audience almost as well as if the viewing screen were not there. This makes it possible for puppets to interact with the audience. Interaction with a puppet is a delightful experience for children. If you are leading a group by yourself it is a distinct advantage to be able to clearly see all who are in the room.

This stage can be made with side panels at right angles to the front panel as shown here. However, if the side panels are spread out a bit so that the back of the stage is wider than the front (see drawing on page 19), there will be more room inside of the stage for the puppeteer.

OPEN-PROSCENIUM STAGE
The proscenium is the area where puppets appear. A conventional window stage is essentially a box with a window cut out—as shown in other drawings. An open-proscenium stage has open space above and at the sides of the puppets. The advantages are much better visibility of the puppets, and both room lighting and stage lighting more fully surround puppets than in a window stage.

DIRECTIONS FOR MAKING FOLDING OPEN-PROSCENIUM STAGE WITH VIEWING SCREEN

NOTE: Dimensions given in drawing are for a small stage that can be used by one adult sitting on a low chair, or a small child standing. Adjust dimensions to your needs. The height of the stage should be at least 1" above the head of the tallest puppeteer using the stage. The height of the proscenium should be about 2" below shoulder height of a puppeteer. For a wider stage, insert another middle panel.

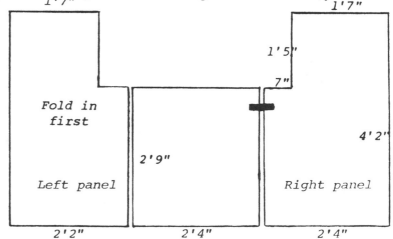

1. *Tape 3 pieces of corrugated cardboard together* as shown in drawing. The left panel is 2" narrower than the right panel so stage can be folded flat for storage. Use 2" wide duct tape (hardware store) and tape the left panel ½" apart from the middle panel. Tape the right pane ¾" apart from the middle panel. Turn stage over and place tape over exposed tape so no sticky tape is exposed (see drawing).

2. *Make and attach scrim curtain* (viewing screen). Perhaps the best choice for scrim material is medium weight polyester jersey. Black is the best color since a lighter color is harder to see through without being seen by the audience. Another choice could be lightweight T-shirt material. When choosing yardage, check for see-through quality. Then, as a test, lay a section of the material over several bolts of yardage. They should not be visible.

Size of scrim: Cut scrim to meansure 50" wide and long enough to hang about 2" below proscenium. Make allowances for top hem (also bottom hem if you wish to add bead weight to bottom of scrim; bead weight is available at yardage stores and helps keep scrib in place). Sew top hem large enough to admit 3/16" diameter dowel (round stick from hardware store).

To attach scrim to stage: Cut holes in top front of stage about 1" from edges and large enough to admit dowel. Set stage upright and position sides as desired— at right angles to front or spread apart. Place dowel through holes. Cut dowel so it will extend 2" past holes. Push dowel through hem in scrim and through holes. If needed, attach clamps or clothespins to ends of dowel to keep dowel in position.

3. *Cover top and back of stage.* Stage must be dark inside or the scrim will not be adequate to conceal puppeteer. Use lightweight, non-see-through cloth. Certain types of inexpensive satin coat lining work well. Hold cloth up to a light source to determine its density. Two layers may be required. Cut holes to admit another 3/16" dowel about 1" from top back edges of stage. Cut dowel to extend 2" past stage. Cut cloth to extend about 3" over sides of stage. Cloth need extend only

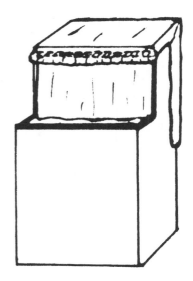

19

a short distance below the level of the proscenium; it need not reach to the floor. Place cloth over top and back of stage and secure with clamps at ends of dowels.

If you prefer to cover top of stage with cardboard: cut cardboard to measure 2½" past top of stage. cut 2" squares from corners of cardboard. Score cardboard 2" from edges and bend to hang over stage. Hand non-see-through cloth from inside back of cardboard roof.

view inside stage

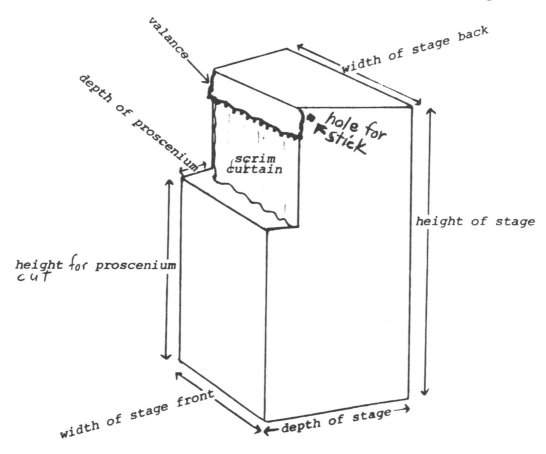

4. *Decorate stage* (optional, but recommended). Contact paper (self-adhesive plastic covering available in variety and hardware stores) is attractive. Choose a design that doesn't draw too much attention to itself and away from the puppets. A brick, rock or wood-grain design is a good choice.

You might want to have children decorate the stage with colored art paper. Have them cut or tear paper in irregular shapes. Glue pieces to stage—start at the bottom and overlap pieces.

5. *Border proscenium cut* (optional, but recommended). Press on 2" wide strips of colored tape; even grey duct tape makes an attractive border. Or glue on 2" wide strips of felt. If children decorate stage you might want to border all edges of the stage.

Puppet Animation

POSITION OF PUPPETEER AND PUPPET

A puppeteer may stand, sit or kneel. If you perform in full view of an audience (not behind a stage) hold the puppet beside you. When using a stage hold the puppet either over your head or in front of your face—depending on the type of stage. Puppeteers who stand and hold puppets overhead have the most mobility. However, for interaction between puppet and audience, and for those who find it difficult to hold their hand overhead for very long, we recommend a stage with a one-way viewing curtain.

POSITION OF YOUR HAND IN PUPPET

The position of your hand in a puppet will depend on the type of puppet you have. The two most common types are illustrated by the drawings. *Movable-mouth puppet* (1st drawing): Place your hand in puppet with four fingers above mouth and thumb below mouth. *Glove puppet* (2nd drawing): Place your thumb in one arm. The position of the rest of your fingers will depend on the size of your fingers, the width of the puppet's neck and arms, and which position allows the best animation. Possibilities: one, two or three fingers in head, and either your little finger or little and ring fingers in other arm.

WALKING

There are several methods of having a puppet walk. You may wish to choose a different walk for each puppet. (1) GLIDE—This is the simplest walk. The puppet smoothly glides across the stage—no up-and-down or sideways movement. (2) HOP— ᴍᴍ . (3) SWOOP—This is the opposite of a hop walk. Lower and raise the puppet for each step ᴜᴜᴜ . (4) LEAN—As the puppet glides, hops or swoops across the stage, he also leans from side to side (as the puppeteer makes a twisting motion with wrist), leaning to one side for the first step and to the other for the second step, etc. (5) Twist—As the puppet glides, hops or swoops across the stage, he also twists.

A dainty puppet would take short steps. A sad puppet would walk slowly. A puppet that takes rapid steps would appear to be running.

MISCELANEOUS ACTIONS

Different types of puppets have different capabilities. See how many of these actions your puppet can perform:

-hang head
-nod head
-hold head with hands
-scratch head
-hold hands over ears
-point
-bow
-wave
-beckon
-cock head to one side to listen
-pat tummy
-stand on head
-lay on back and hang head over stage
-quiver (tighten the muscles in your arm and make your whole arm tremble)
-tip head from side to side (mouth puppet: press down with little finger, then press down with index finger, alternating fingers)
-shake head,"No" (glove puppet: roll neck tube against another finger or twist two fingers)
-smile (place little fingers and

thumb in lower mouth, press up with thumb and little finger, press down with three middle fingers; if an animal puppet has a long nose, you may be able to pull the upper mouth back a bit to simulate a smile)

-frown (puppet with flexible mouth: place thumb at center of lower mouth; press down with little finger and index finger in upper mouth)

ROD ATTACHED TO PUPPET'S ARM (PAW) TO ASSIST ACTIONS

If you wish to attach a rod to a puppet's arm or paw: Attach a screw eye (size 215½) to one end of a 24" bamboo garden stake (used to support plants). To help you grasp the other end, wrap tape round and round until it is about ½" thick. Sew the screw eye to the palm of the puppet's arm (paw). If desired, cover the screw eye with same fabric used for puppet.

Or, instead of a stake, straighten a section of coat hanger wire, bend one end into a small loop and use glue to close any space left at end of loop. Pin or sew loop to wrist or palm of puppet's hand. Another method for coat hanger wire is to make a loop 1" from the end; open the stitching at the lower side of the puppet's wrist; insert wire so loop is just inside the puppet's arm; sew loop to puppet. Instead of wrapping tape around the wire to form a grasp, you can bend the wire as shown.

ANIMATION DO'S AND DON'TS

Look at the image of your puppet in a mirror. Have the puppet demonstrate all of the following DO'S and DON'TS. Once you see how the DON'TS come across to an audience, try not to repeat these mistakes.

1. *Entrances and exits.* DO: If stage has side curtains, have the puppet enter and exit via curtains. Otherwise, enter as if climbing stairs, either facing audience or sideways. Exit as if decending stairs, with back or side to audience. Enter and exit at either side of stage or midstage. DON'T: Pop the puppet up and down or have it "ride an elevator" up and down—unless you are not concerned about the believability of a performance.
2. *Height.* DO: Establish a "floor" for puppets (the audience does); maintain this height. DON'T: Sink through the floor or rise above the floor.
3. *Posture.* DO: Stand up straight (except animals with a neck that naturally leans forward). DON'T: Lean on stage, lean or bend forward, backwards or sidewards.
4. *Movements.* DO: Make clear, deliberate, *realistic* movements. DON'T: Make quick, sharp, frantic movements. Don't move constantly. On the other hand, don't freeze—moving not at all or making only minimal movements.
5. *Eye-contact.*
    a) When speaking to an audience. DO: Look at the audience. DON'T: Look over their heads, at the ceiling, at the side wall or at the floor.
    b) When speaking to another puppet. DO: Look at the eyes of the puppet—except for occasional glances at the audience. DON'T: Look over the other puppet's head, at his mid-section, at his feet or off to the side.
    c) When looking at an object. DO: Look at the object. DON'T: Look anyplace else.
    NOTE: Some puppets can not make good eye-contact unless you bend your wrist down at what may seem to be an uncomfortable position—at least at first.
6. *When another puppet speaks.* DO: Respond to the puppet talking, but keep movements to a minimum—so the audience doesn't have to figure out who is talking. DON'T: "Steal the show"—unless the script indicates hyperactivity.
7. *Impossible tasks*—closing eyes, passing an object, etc. DO: Face away from the audience and leave the action to the audience's imagination. Or exit briefly—with

silence indicating the action, or with an offstage voice(s) describing action. Or have a narrator describe more involved activity. DON'T: Face the audience, making the inability obvious.

ADJUSTMENTS FOR PROBLEM PUPPETS

If your puppet has one or more of the following problems, here are some suggested solutions.

1. *Puppet too narrow to fit on your arm.* Slit sides or back of puppet. If needed, sew on triangular piece of material—to cover slit.
2. *Puppet too short to cover enough of your arm.* Make the puppet longer by sewing on a piece of identical or contrasting material. Or attach a flared or gathered skirt, or pants, to the puppet. For pants separation, see "Overgarments," under *Basic Pattern,* this chapter.
3. *Puppet's mouth won't stay closed without pressure from your hand.* This is usually due to a cardboard backing that was not designed to fold over a felt mouth. Try placing a pencil at the fold of the mouth and crushing the cardboard over the pencil. If this doesn't work, turn puppet inside out (or reach inside puppet) and very carefully use razor blade to cut partway through cardboard. If fold needs reinforcing, place plastic or cloth tape over fold—be sure to have mouth completely closed when adding tape.
4. *Foam-head puppet has mouth that doesn't open easily.* Foam that extends too far down back of puppet's head may restrict mouth openings. Fold such foam inside head to see if this relieves pressure. Also foam around mouth corners can be a problem. You may want to tear or cut mouth corner foam. Any mistakes in tearing or cutting can be repaired with contact cement (use original type, not water-soluble type).
5. *Puppet gradually slips off your hand during a performance.* You can: a) Place stuffing between the back of your hand and the puppet. b) Hold bottom of puppet (either in front or in back) with your free hand. If puppet is short, you might want to attach a string or ribbon to bottom of puppet to hold onto. c) If your elbow will be bent when working puppet, sew loop of elastic inside back of puppet. Place your hand through loop first, then into puppet (see drawing at right).

    Or you may find that all you need to do is glue a finger-grasp to upper portion of puppet's mouth. Glue on 3 or more 2"x1" layers of corrugated cardboard in position shown in drawing—just behind your fingertips. Or cut a 1-3/4"x5" strip of cereal box cardboard, or longer strip of felt. Roll up tight and glue closed—secure with tape or pin until glue is dry. Glue roll to mouth. If puppet doesn't have cardboard backing on its mouth, you can add a finger-grasp to cardboard, then glue cardboard to puppet's mouth. A good finger-grasp for this type of mouth is to cut three pieces of felt, each 2"x1", and use needle and thread or sewing machine to sew felt to cardboard. Place felt pieces in a pile and sew down middle.

6. *Puppet's head doesn't feel snug on your hand and mouth doesn't respond well to the opening and closing of your hand.* METHOD #1: Stuff puppet wherever needed (head, nose, chin, back of neck, etc.). For stuffing use crumpled paper toweling, Dacron pillow stuffing, cotton (cooler than Dacron), nylon hose (may be shredded), or polyfoam (solid pieces or shreds). If stuffing won't stay in place by itself, or if it irritates your hand, sew stuffing into small cloth bag. Sew or glue bag to puppet. Sew two or three stitches through a seam or other inconspicuous place. Thick, white craft glue works well. (Do not press hard on any glued areas.)

    METHOD #2: Turn puppet inside out. Cut 2 pieces of cereal box, shoe box or corrugated cardboard—one to fit upper mouth and one to fit lower mouth. Glue or

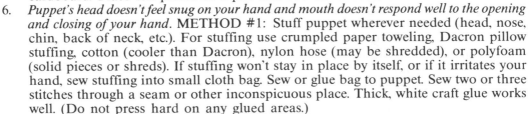

sew on a 3/4" wide strip of cardboard or elastic, leaving room for fingers and thumb. Place strip at straight edge of upper mouth, and far enough down on lower mouth to fit over tip of your thumb (not past thumb joint). Glue cardboard mouth pieces to original mouth. If puppet's mouth is felt or cloth, spread glue on cardboard and press cardboard gently onto felt—so glue will not seep through felt. DO NOT get glue on felt mouth where it folds, as glue will not dry sufficiently  pliable. If mouth fold needs reinforcing, attach plastic or cloth tape—do this when mouth is completely closed. If a cardboard strip needs reinforcing, glue sturdy cloth on top.

If puppet can't be turned inside out, estimate size and cut cardboard mouth. Do not cut separate upper and lower mouth. Fold cardboard along broken lines, making two folds (see drawing at right). Insert mouth into puppet to test size. Make another if necessary. Spread thin layer of glue inside cardboard mouth. Hold mouth in your hand and insert into puppet's head. Use fingers of hand holding cardboard to help open cardboard mouth. Place your free hand in felt mouth to help position felt on cardboard. Do not press hard on glued area. Open mouth wide and lightly press felt against cardboard—felt should reach, or almost reach, cardboard at fold at back of mouth.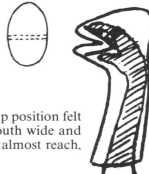

Making Puppets Speak

VOICES FOR PUPPETS

When speaking for a puppet you'll want to change your voice if the audience can see both you and the puppet. If you're out of sight, change your voice if your natural voice doesn't fit the puppet's personality or if your voice is well-known to the audience. Look at the image of your puppet in a mirror and experiment with different voices (see suggestions below).

1. *Vary your voice pitch.* Try these four voice changes: a) Use your normal method of speaking but pitch your voice a couple of notes higher than is customary for you. b) Pitch your voice a couple of notes higher still—but not high enough to be squeaky as a squeaky voice soon becomes irritating to an audience. c) Pitch your voice a little lower than usual. d) Pitch your voice lower still.
2. *Speak faster or slower than is normal for you,* but not so fast that you can't be understood nor so slow that your audience loses interest.
3. *Modify English.* Speak with a foreign accent, Southern dialect, cowboy jargon, etc. Or speak as if you had a cold or an allergy problem.
4. *Modulate excessively.* Make your voice go high and low more often and to a greater extent than usual. This makes a good little girl voice—especially if you force out a little extra air when speaking, and gasp when taking a breath.
5. *Speak monotonously.* Speak in an unvaried key or style—perhaps saying words in a monotone and slurring your voice down on the last syllable of each phrase or sentence.
6. *Use a stage whisper.* Project your voice well and speak in a LOUD whisper. If a man doesn't have a good falsetto he can simulate a female voice this way.
7. *Purse your lips.* Push your lips out as far as possible and leave them pushed out as you speak. Give special attention to good enunciation.
8. *Drop your jaw.* Drop your jaw down as far as possible for each syllable of speech.

9. *Tighten your throat muscles to produce a raspy voice.* Caution: this can result in a sore throat if used too long at a time.
10. *Hold your nose.* Hold your nose as you speak with a relaxed throat. Or hold you nose as you speak with a tensed throat.
11. *Pinch your cheek and hold it far out.* Or place a washed pebble in your cheek.
12. *Speak with your normal voice while pushing more air out of your mouth.*
13. *Speak in short (2 or 3 word) phrases, and pause between phrases.* Young child.
14. *Combinations of the above.* After you have mastered one type of voice change you might want to combine this with another change. If you are speaking slower than is normal for you, try (at the same time) pitching your voice higher, etc.
15. *Listen to voices for TV cartoon characters, including the Charlie Brown gang.*
  NOTE: Use true-to-life voices (not comical voices) for Christian-story characters.

THE IMPORTANCE OF "LIPSYNC"

"Lipsync" is the synchronization of a puppet's mouth movements with the words being spoken. Good lipsync is essential for a good puppet presentation. Watching a puppet with poor lipsync is like watching a motion picture that is out of "sync" with the sound system.

Good lipsync is not difficult to learn, but may take concentrated effort in the beginning. These instructions are not meant to be complicated. Read them for the basic ideas. With practice, good lipsync will become automatic and you won't have to think about a puppet's mouth movements.

LOOK AT THE IMAGE OF YOUR PUPPET IN A MIRROR AS YOU FOLLOW THESE INSTRUCTIONS

DO NOT "BITE" WORDS. The tendency of many beginners is to bite words with a puppet's mouth. To learn what it is to bite words: silently open a puppet's mouth. Now close the mouth as you say "How." Silently open, then close as you say "are." Open...close as you say "you." Open. . .close as you say "to." Open. . .close as you say "day?" Slowly repeat the words, "How are you today?" biting each word (or syllable). Now that you know what it is to bite words, try NEVER to do it again.

START SPEAKING AS SOON AS YOU START TO OPEN A PUPPET'S MOUTH. If you do this you won't bite words. Slowly open your hand; start saying "How" as soon as you start to open and continue saying "How" until your hand is fully open. Now close your hand. Open again slowly as you say "are;" then close. Do the same for the rest of the sentence.

CLOSE A PUPPET'S MOUTH WHEN THE PUPPET ISN'T SPEAKING. Close a puppet's mouth immediately after each word (syllable) is spoken. After you finish saying "How," do not hesitate before closing the puppet's mouth. Also, after a puppet finishes a speech, do not reopen the mouth until the puppet has something else to say—unless the puppet is gawking, showing surprise, showing disbelief or yawning.

WIDTH OF MOUTH OPENINGS. When first learning lipsync, it is helpful to speak slowly and open a puppet's mouth wide for each syllable. After you get the feeling for lipsync, you will probably want to open a puppet's mouth about halfway for normal speech, leaving the widest openings for exclamations, loud calling, etc.

FASTER SPEECH. Open and close a puppet's mouth for each syllable as much as possible. But when you can't keep up, combine some syllables and short words.

The easiest way to start practicing combining syllables is to use only one mouth opening and closing for each word—not for each syllable as for slow speech. After you get the feeling for this, also combine words that naturally go together. For instance: say "I am going to town" with three mouth openings and closings (*I am-going to-town*). You will

25

instinctively know which words to combine as you practice. After practicing combining syllables and words, give attention to dividing long words into more than one mouth opening and closing—for more realistic lipsync. A word such as "Minneapolis" can be divided into three openings and closings (*Minne-apo-lis*) or, for more rapid speech, into two openings and closings (*Minne-apolis*).

CAUTION: Combine syllables and words only when necessary—when you can't keep up. A puppet's mouth should not appear to be "flapping" without regard to the words spoken. Neither should a mouth move in a predictable rhythmic pattern without regard to the words spoken.

PRACTICE WORKS FOR SUCCESS

Practice voices. Practice switching back and forth from your normal voice to the puppet voice until it seems natural to change your voice when speaking for the puppet. If you will be using more than one puppet, develop a different voice for each one.

A good exercise is to read a newspaper aloud and change your voice for each new sentence. Either alternate your voice and a puppet voice, or alternate two puppet voices. When alternating two puppet voices it might be helpful to think: high/low; fast/slow; modulate/monotone; tight throat and high voice/drop jaw; loud whisper/purse lips; etc.

Project your voice. Words have no value if they cannot be heard. To avoid the common problem of speaking too softly, project your voice. Do not shout out words; instead, take a breath and force the air out of your throat by pushing in with your strong stomach muscles. Now speak as you push in. Relax your throat and let your voice float out. (Tense your throat only when doing a voice that requires a tight throat.)

Enunciate well. Words have no value if they cannot be understood. Do not speak with "lazy lips" and do not "swallow" words. The most common problem is swallowing the ends of words. Give attention to pronouncing the final sound as clearly as the first.

Practice lipsync. Sing: A good way to practice lipsync in the beginning is to have your puppet sing, holding each note for a prolonged period. Keep your hand open as long as you are holding a note. *Speak:* While watching the puppet in a mirror, have the puppet say something you have committed to memory. Carefully observe the puppet's mouth movements. *Watch Sesame Street:* Watch, and try to imitate, the mouth-movements of the Sesame Street puppets. It'd be hard to find a better teacher.

Ask for evaluation. Besides evaluating a puppet's image in a mirror, ask people to comment on your use of voices and the puppet's lipsync. Choose those who will give an honest report.

Don't let flubs fluster you. It's easy for a beginner to forget and use the wrong voice when speaking for a puppet. If this happens you can simply ignore the mistake and change to the correct voice. Or you might have the puppet say, "Hey, why am I talking like this? (AFTER CHANGING TO CORRECT VOICE) I'm supposed to talk like this." (CONTINUE SPEAKING IN CORRECT VOICE)

Beginners. It might be better to master lipsync and animation before trying voices.

Making and Using Signs for Props

Throughout the book you will find references to various types of props. You will be told how to have a puppet appear to be fishing with a fishing pole, how a puppet can hold a note in his mouth, and even what happens when he loses it. Most of the props are in the form of signs; therefore, details about making and using signs will be helpful here as you put your puppets in action.

VARIETY OF SIGNS

Using a variety of types of signs adds interest to puppet presentations. Several types of signs and sign supports are described here. If you do not have materials on hand for making one type, you may find that another type will do just as well.

PRINTING FOR SIGNS

Printing for signs used with children usually should be the same style taught in local schools. You may need to adapt the printing in the samples accordingly. Crayon can be used, but wide-tip felt pens are recommended because of their intense sharp lines. Black is the best color for signs, but other deep and medium colors can also be effective. If children will be handling felt pens, use the watercolor type. For fancy shading of letters, etc., observe signs in stores. Test the readability of all signs by sitting in the last row of seating to view a sign.

HOW TO DISPLAY A SIGN DURING A PRESENTATION

If a sign is to appear during (not before) a session, consider these alternatives:

Veiled Sign. Set the sign in place beforehand and cover it with a cloth. The puppeteer, or puppet using his hands or mouth, unveils the sign at the proper time.

Puppet-manipulated Sign. If a puppet is not capable of holding or placing a sign in position, hold the puppet near the sign as the puppeteer moves it; this will make the puppet appear to be manipulating the sign.

Puppet-controlled Sign. When a puppet gives a request or a command, a sign obeys and enters, moves, or exits, seemingly without assistance. If the hand of the puppeteer will be seen moving a sign, give the hand a name, such as *Handy,* and have the puppet give *Handy* directions. Cover *Handy* with a decorative garden glove or fuzzy mitten and attach a sleeve of cloth to the glove, to conceal the puppeteer's arm, in case it also shows above the stage.

Mischievous sign behavior. Signs by themselves, or *Handy,* might occasionally be mischievous and need to be spoken to two or three times before obeying, or they might act contrary to instructions. A forgetful *Handy* might appear without a sign and have to go to look for it. A limited amount of mischievous sign behavior could be added to the skits in this book and written into original skits.

NOTE: A sign in motion is difficult to read. Be sure that a sign is held perfectly still long enough to be read.

SIGNBOARD

A signboard is covered with decorative material and serves as a mount for Bible verses printed on paper. To change the sign, simply change Bible verses.

Material for signboards. Corrugated cardboard makes excellent signboards because pins can be pushed through a temporary sign into the cardboard. However, temporary signs can be taped or clipped easily to signboards made of sturdy paper, paper sacks or lightweight cardboard (i.e. cereal boxes).

Covering for signboards. Felt, burlap, flannel, or other solid-color cloth works nicely. If signs will be taped (not pinned) to a signboard, solid-color contact paper makes an attractive covering because tape is easily removed from contact paper. If desired, a sign can be attached invisibly with loops of tape (sticky side out) on back of sign.

Make a border of contrasting color felt, colored tape, paper or contact paper. If, on occasion, a temporary sign completely covers a signboard, make a border around the paper sign. Experiment with borders (width, materials, positions) on scrap paper before making your final sign.

SHEET SIGN

A sheet sign is simply a sheet of paper, sturdy paper bag, file folder or piece of cardboard, either with or without a display handle. If sign does not have handle, do not print close to bottom edge, as entire sign will not show above stage.

Handle: (Handle will support cardboard sign 18"x 24" or larger.) Bend 1-1/2" wide strip of cardboard so center portion extends away from sign just far enough for fingers to grasp handle. Sew, glue, or use paper fasteners to attach handle to sign slightly above center, or at center if sign is to be revolved. (To revolve sign: use finger movement as for twirling a baton.) If sign will not be revolved and will be held above stage level, cloth can be attached to hide puppeteer's hand. Handle for lightweight paper sign can be paper folded and taped on.

FOLDED SIGN

Use typing paper, shelf paper, butcher paper, art paper or piece cut from paper bag. Glue pieces together for larger sign.

To Make Folded Sign: Fold paper, file folder or cardboard to fit over edge of stage. Puppeteer's hand will not be seen placing sign in position if sign is folded so portion inside stage is longer than portion placed over stage. (If necessary, to accommodate thickness of stage, make two folds at top of sign.)

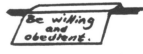

Tape; Rings. If cardboard is too stiff to remain in folded position: (1) cut across top fold(s), (2) tape pieces together 1/4" apart (see first drawing at right), placing tape on both sides of sign so no sticky tape remains exposed. Or join pieces with rings (see second drawing at right).

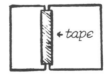

GROCERY-BAG SIGN

Fold any size grocery bag flat and hang over stage, either with bottom of bag facing audience or bottom of bag inside stage.

Thick stage. If stage is thick, and bottom of bag faces audience, fold bag as shown in first drawing at right.

If side of bag faces audience, fold as shown in second drawing at right. To provide *weight* so bag will not fall forward off stage, fold identical bag in half and glue or staple to sign bag in position shown by shaded area in second drawing. If extra stiffening is needed to hold sign bag in position on stage: cut small box (such as container for plastic sandwich bags) in half diagonally, or use two corners of larger box. Then staple or glue box piece(s) to sign bag in position shown in second drawing.

Grocery-bag signboard. A paper sign can be attached to a grocery bag signboard in either a sideways or upright position. For larger signs, staple, glue or tape two pieces of paper together and attach to bag. Paper will extend past bag.

STICK SIGN

To make stick sign, staple, glue, or tape sheet sign to handle (stick, ruler, paint paddle, yardstick, dowel, plastic pipe, cardboard tube from pants hanger, or two or more strips of cardboard glued together). If handle will be seen, cover with paint, felt, contact paper, or cloth.

When using tape,

spacer   bracket

to protect back of sign from repeated removal of tape, place one or more strips of permanent tape to back of sign (use wide tape or two strips of narrow tape overlapped). Use narrow tape to attach handle to sign.

Spacer for stick sign: So that sign will rest on stage unattended, glue strips of corrugated cardboard between sign and stick (make strips wider than stick but not as wide as sign; number of strips depends on thickness of stage). Second spacer placed near top of sign will keep sign straight. Large sign may need two sticks, placed several inches apart, so sign will not tip sideways. A heavy sign may fall forward off stage unless stick is extra long or weight is attached to bottom of stick, or both.

"Bracket" For Stick Signs: So sign will rest on stage and be held higher than sign with spacer, glue strips of corrugated cardboard to stick (make strips wider than stick if stability is needed). Make last strip longer. Cover bracket with material that matches

stage. Large sign may need two sticks, each with bracket—to keep sign from tipping sideways.

REVOLVING STICK SIGN

Drill hole through wood or cardboard stick near one end. Poke hole through center of circular piece of cardboard or sturdy paper. Attach sign to stick with bolt and nut or long paper fastener. To assist in revolving the sign, make tabs by gluing popsicle sticks or strips of cardboard to back of sign, as shown in drawing. If tabs restrict turning of sign by catching on the stick, cut piece of paper the same size as sign and place on back of sign. The paper will cover tabs and keep them from catching on the stick.

If a revolving sign will be hand-held, it needs no bracket. If it is to rest on stage, a bracket such as described above will be needed.

The sign is revolved by person outside theater, by puppet using hands or mouth, or by puppeteer using *Handy* or lowering sign so hand won't be seen.

SWINGING STICK SIGN

At times making a sign swing can add a bit of fun to a presentation. After a sign swings a little while, a puppet can declare that it's difficult to read a moving sign. A puppet might have to stand in the way to stop a swinging sign. Such periods of misbehavior should be short.

Sign with limited swing. Slip stick inside folded grocery bag. To keep stick in place, staple bag together on both sides of stick near top, but not so close that motion is restricted. To increase movement, slit sides of bag and tape down any side folds that interfere with movement of bag.

Sign with full swing. Drill hole through stick near one end. Poke hole through piece of cardboard or folded grocery bag near top center of sign. If fold of grocery bag interferes with swing, tape to bag. Attach sign to stick with bolt and nut or paper fastener.

STANDS FOR SIGNS

A sign not supported by hand or stage will need a means of support. Instructions are given for making short stands which can be placed on the stageboard, risers for some short stands, and tall stands, which are preferable in some situations.

Short stands for sheet signs:

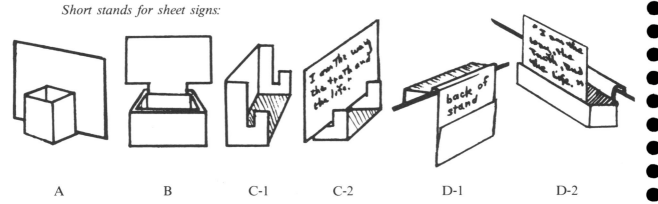

A   B   C-1   C-2   D-1   D-2

30

A. *ONE-BOX STAND*. Glue small box to back of sign. Place weight in box.
B. *TWO-BOX STAND*. Place smaller box, or pillow, inside larger box. Place sign between boxes, or between pillow and box. Place weight in box if needed.
C. *SLOT STAND*. Cut end off cardboard box and cut as shown in drawing C-1 making slot just large enough for sign to slide into. Sign should stand upright (C-2) for easy visibility from audience. If cardboard in front of sign hides view of printing, cut it shorter. To keep sign from falling forward: tie knot in end of string, sew knot to back of sign and wind string around button sewed to back of stand (see drawing C-3).

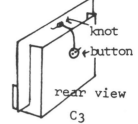

D. *BOX AND BAG STAND*. Cut lid off aluminum foil box or plastic wrap box. Or cut 3" section off large cereal box (shown by shaded area in drawing D-1.) Staple or glue box to large-size grocery bag, attaching bag to top of sack (bottom of bag hangs inside stage). Fold sack over stage, making two folds to accommodate width of stage. Note, in drawing D-2 that sign is at front of box. To keep sign upright, place stuffing (crumpled paper sack, lightweight cardboard box) either behind, or in front of, sign.

Short stands for stick signs:

Sign sticks can be inserted and removed easily from any of the stands shown. The stands will support larger signs and longer sticks than those indicated in the drawings.

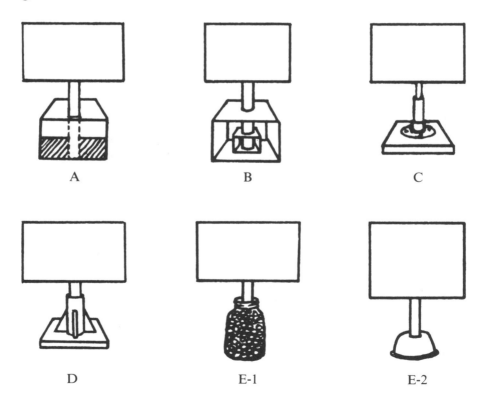

A. *ONE-BOX STAND* (for sign with flat stick). Push box flaps firmly against inside of box; turn box upside down. Cut slot same size as sign stick at one edge of bottom of box. Push stick through slot and between flap and inside of box. Weight top of box if needed.

B. *TWO-BOX STAND.* Push all box flaps inside. Cut slot size of stick through center of one side of both boxes. Place smaller box inside larger box. Push stick through both holes. Position smaller box so sign stands upright; glue smaller box to larger box. Weight box if needed.

C. *PLASTIC-PIPE STAND.* Cut short length of plastic pipe (pipe should be just wide enough to admit sign stick). Screw metal flange to piece of board or plywood. Screw plastic adapter into flange; push pipe into adapter. (Many hardware stores carry plastic pipe.)

D. *CARDBOARD-TUBE STAND.* Place cardboard tube (or cardboard formed into a tube) on wood base. Position 4 triangles of wood, angle irons or shelf brackets firmly against cardboard; attach (glue, tape, screw) to wood and cardboard.

E. *CONTAINER STANDS.* (E-1) Fill glass jar, flower vase, cardboard box or tin can with dry beans or gravel. If container has no lid: cut one from plastic or cardboard; cut stick-size hole in center; tape lid to container.

(E-2) Use cardboard or plastic container for soft margerine, cottage cheese, whipped topping or ice cream. Turn container upside down; use sharp knife to cut stick-size hole in bottom. To cut slot for flat stick, cut the two longer lines first. Place strong tape over unintentional cuts. Fill container with dry beans; tape lid in place. If hole is too large, place layers of tape around hole or glue popsicle sticks to stick.

If more stability is needed, cut circle of sturdy cardboard to fit about 1" inside container; use lid for pattern but cut ¼" to ½" inside tracing line. Cut stick-size hole in center of cardboard. With container right side up and stick through hole, fill with dry beans to level of cardboard; place cardboard over stick; fill with beans to level of lid; tape lid to container.

Plaster of Paris (from hardware store), instead of dry beans, used in the container will support larger and heavier sign.

Use for mold: containers suggested above; cardboard box; paper sack with top folded down or cut off; or cereal box (side cut out, top stapled or taped in position). To save on amount of plaster needed for broad base, set narrow mold in broad mold.

Directions: Mix plaster, using minimum water. Pour and spoon plaster into mold. Wash mixing utensils. When plaster begins to set (knife scrapes surface), insert stick (pole). If plaster doesn't support stick (pole), try again in 30 seconds or so.

If hole in plaster is desired—so stick (pole) can be inserted and removed when desired—insert and remove clean dry stick (pole) periodically until hole remains intact. Do not leave stick (pole) in hole until plaster has dried overnight.

If paper sack or cardboard box is used for mold, set stand on wire rack to dry.

If stick (pole) sets slanted in stand, prop up one side so sign will be upright.

RISERS FOR SHORT STANDS

If your stage has a stageboard (shelf), short stands can be placed on stageboard.
Otherwise, all short stands (except box and bag stand) require a riser.

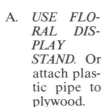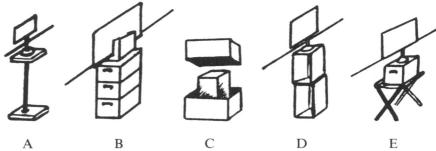

A. *USE FLO-RAL DIS-PLAY STAND.* Or attach plas-tic pipe to plywood.
Pipe can be 1/2" or larger in diameter. Attach adapters to pipe. Screw adapters into metal flanges that have been screwed to plywood (perhaps 8" square base and 6" top. Plywood need be only thick enough to admit screws.

B. *CARDBOARD BOXES.* Set boxes on their sides; place weights in boxes if needed. Or set boxes right side up, either with flaps overlapped or glued shut (fill boxes with crumpled newspapers to aid in gluing flaps). Glue boxes together if desired. To make handles for easy carrying, cut slots in sides of boxes.

C. *THREE IDENTICAL BOXES.* Wedge boxes together for extra stability. Fold all flaps inside. Force middle box into bottom box. Weight lower box if needed. Force top box over middle box. Add fourth box on top if needed for height.

D. *WOODEN BOXES SET ON END.*

E. *BOX ON TOP OF TV TRAY.*

TALL STANDS FOR SIGNS

Tall stands, rather than short stands, are preferable in some situations. All drawings show rear view of stands.

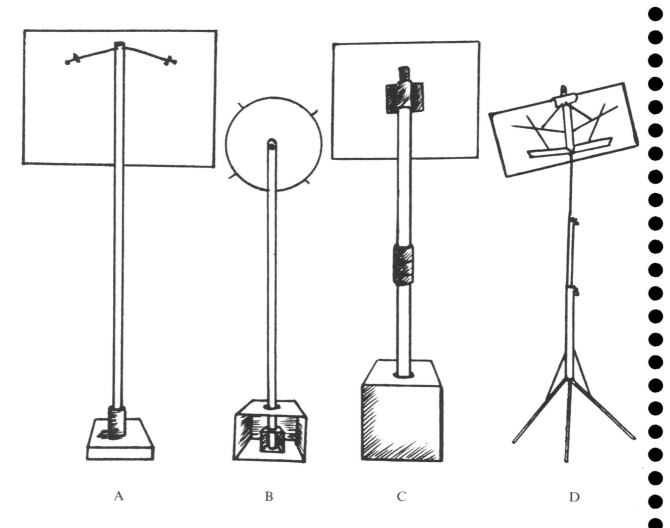

A   B   C   D

A. *PLASTIC PIPE IN PLASTER; STRING SIGNBOARD.* Cement plastic pipe coupling to one end of 4" length of 3/4" thin-wall plastic pipe. Fill 8"x8" cardboard box with 2" Plaster of Paris (directions above). Insert (do not cement) 6' length of 3/4" thin-wall plastic pipe into coupling. Set 4" end of pipe in plaster. Prop plastic pipe upright (tie to three chairs) to keep straight until plaster sets. Poke string through holes punched in 24"x30" cardboard signboard; tie string. Saw notches in end of 6' pipe; hang sign on notches. NOTE: 6' length of plastic pipe can be cemented to coupling if desired, but will not then be removable for storage. Plastic pipe can be cut easily with a hack saw.

B. *MOP HANDLE IN TWO-BOX STAND; REVOLVING SIGN.* Drill hole in one end of mop handle (push-broom handle for taller stand); attach sign with bolt and nut. Set mop handle in two-box stand; weight stand. (Aluminum tubing can be used instead of wood pole.)

C. *YARDSTICKS IN ONE-BOX STAND; POCKET SIGNBOARD.* Lay yardstick on 20"x22" cardboard sign. Just above center of sign bend two strips of cardboard around yardstick to form pocket for yardstick. Glue pocket strips to each other and to sign. Overlap two yardsticks to desired height and tape yardsticks together (or hold in place with large metal clips). Set lower yardstick in one-box stand (8"x11"x13" or larger). Slip sign pocket over yardstick.

D. *SIGNBOARD CLIPPED TO MUSIC STAND.* Clip (or tape) 12"x20" cardboard sign to *back* side of music stand. Sign slants downward, but this is an advantage as audience is usually below sign. If sign is placed where sheet of music would rest, prop and tape to stand upright.

E. *CHRISTMAS TREE STAND (not shown)* Attach small frozen juice can to Christmas tree stand. Place pole (plastic pipe, mop handle, etc.) in can; pad can if pole tilts.

NOTE: Folded sign or grocery-bag sign can be placed over signboard attached to "A" or "C."

3

Friend Puppets
Work in the Church

Friend puppets can be very busy little personalities in the Sunday School and other activities around the church. Here are some good ideas and scripts ready to use. Then you can take them as idea starters and write scripts of your own.

Friend Puppet Welcomes

It is important to welcome visitors to Sunday School and other activities, and to make regular attenders feel welcome and loved. Following are some good ways to do it.

GREET CHILDREN AT DOOR
Young children will look forward to having a puppet welcome them and converse with them at vthe door.

Position of puppeteer. The puppeteer can be in view or in an enclosed theater with a viewing screen.

Puppet's attitude toward children. Do not have a puppet be aggressive toward a small child. The puppet can even be more shy than the child is.

Have a puppet talk about how much he likes children and how much fun it is to talk to boys and girls. A puppet might whisper a secret in each child's ear "I love you" or "I'm sure glad you came today." A puppet may give and receive head pats, hand shakes or kisses—depending on the type of puppet used and the child's choice.

Topics of conversation. Suggested questions: "What did you see on the way to church today?" "What did you have for breakfast?" (Puppet might comment that he had rocks or mustard.) "What is your favorite Bible story (or Sunday School song)?" "What did you do this past week?. . .It's such fun to hear what kids do." "Do you know where I was all week? In the bottom of the puppet box with a whole bunch of puppets on top of me (groan). Do I look squashed?" "I'm sure glad to be here today. Are you?"

RECOGNIZE EACH CHILD IN A GROUP (one puppet)

PUPPET: Hi, kids. Sunday School is sure the best place to be on Sunday morning. Do you know why this is a great place? It's because we have fun, and we sing, and best of all, we learn about Jesus.

Who's here today? Let's see . . .there's Susie . . .and John is here. . .and Sally's sitting next to Mary. (The puppet might also tell the teacher the names of those present.)

Comments and questions. As each name is mentioned, the puppet might make a comment or ask a question concerning clothing, sitting straight, or recent illness or trip.

Fun things. Children will think it fun if a puppet makes mistakes concerning the color of clothes they are wearing, who they're sitting next to, where they live, etc.

Another fun idea is to have each child tell his name to a puppet; then have the puppet cover his eyes (turn his back) and try to say the names. The children will be delighted when the puppet can't remember all the names at first. He may even forget the teacher's name: "Mrs. —a-a-a. . .kids, what's her name?"

If there is time, have the puppet ask the children to switch places when he turns his back to them. Then, while looking at the children, the puppet would say the names with difficulty.

Children will also be amused if a puppet makes mistakes counting them.

RECOGNIZE EACH CHILD IN A GROUP (two puppets)

#1: (SINGS OR HUMS)
#2: Why are you so happy?
#1: Because so many of my friends came to Sunday School today. (LOOKING AT GROUP) I see Johnny and Alice and Sam. If you'd stayed home, I wouldn't have the fun of seeing you. (TALKS TO THOSE 3)
#2: And look who else is here! (NAMES 2 OR 3 CHILDREN AND CONVERSES WITH THEM)
(CONTINUE ROUTINE UNTIL ALL CHILDREN HAVE BEEN RECOGNIZED)

CONVERSE WITH GROUP

One third-grade superintendent reports: "Puppets can be very successful at gaining attention, stimulating interest, and waking up the group at the start of the hour." For a wake-up, and to make the boys and girls feel welcome, she has a puppet engage the children in informal conversation for a few minutes, asking about their week's activities.

WELCOME GROUP AS A WHOLE

PUPPET: Hi, kids. . .How are you all? When I count to three, how about all of you at the same time, whispering, "Hello, my name is...........Ready. . .one. . .two. . .three. (GROUP RESPONDS) Welcome to all of you. (IF DISCIPLINE IS LIKELY TO BE A PROBLEM, PROCEED IMMEDIATELY INTO ANOTHER ACTIVITY.) Now that we've all said, "Hello," let's sing (name of song). (SONG LEADER TAKES OVER; PUPPET SINGS APPROPRIATE* SONG WITH GROUP, OR KEEPS TIME TO MUSIC, OR EXITS.)

*The difference between *puppet songs* and *people songs* is explained in Chapter 9.

WELCOME TREAT

PUPPET: (EXAGGERATED, FUN-TYPE CRYING) Boo-hoo-hoo-hoo-hoo-waa-waa.
TEACHER: What's wrong?
PUPPET: I want to welcome everybody to Sunday School, but I can't until I find what I lost.
TEACHER: What did you lose?
PUPPET: My sack of popcorn (peanuts, crackers, pumpkin seeds). Boo-hoo-hoo-waa-waa.
TEACHER: Hold on, maybe we can help. Where do you think it might be?
PUPPET: I don't know. I looked all over in the puppet house.
TEACHER: Maybe it's out here somewhere.
PUPPET: It might be. Does anybody see a sack of popcorn? (IF SACK IS NOT IN VIEW, OR EASILY FOUND, TEACHER AND PUPPET GIVE HINTS.)
TEACHER: (AFTER POPCORN IS FOUND) Say, what's finding your popcorn got to do with welcoming the boys and girls?
PUPPET: I want everybody to have a welcome yum-yum. (AS POPCORN IS BEING DISTRIBUTED) Yum-yum. . .good-good. . .welcome—welcome. . .yum-yum. . .

WELCOME VISITORS WITH POP-UP PUPPET

When one or more children knock on the lid of the stage,* puppet pops out, asks the child's name and perhaps gives a handshake, then jumps down to the bottom of the box for a welcome button or other memento. (Or puppet leaves the stage—through back door—takes a button in his hands or mouth from teacher or a box, and returns to give button to the visitor. Or puppet asks teacher to give the button to the visitor.)

Stage: large take-home chicken bucket, cardboard paint bucket or cardboard box. Cover stage with cloth, paper or paint.

GREET WITH A LARGE HUMAN-ARM PUPPET

One Sunday School that uses a human-arm friendly monster puppet reports: "He's the one that greets all the visitors each week, gives each a small treat, shakes hands, and receives many gooey kisses and many, many hugs. He's so loved it's pathetic!

WAKE-UP BEFORE A WELCOME
(Poem may be sung to an original tune.)

PUPPET: I hope you like my face.
I know you'll like this place.
And now I say
That come what may
(SPEAKING ENTHUSIASTICALLY) There's no better place to be right now than (name of church or activity).
Now I shall repeat my beautiful home-made poem and see if you can say the last part. (PUPPET REPEATS POEM, STOPPING AT NAME OF CHURCH OR ACTIVITY)
And who's here today?. . .There's John. . .and I see Alice. . .and there's Ray (OR IF GROUP IS LARGE: I see a whole bunch of third-graders, and just look at all those first-graders. . .) Welcome to all of you.

And now I want to give a special welcome to you visitors. Would all the visitors please stand? (PUPPET CONDUCTS WELCOMING PROCEDURE)

INTRODUCING WELCOME SONG

PUPPET: It's that time again.
TEACHER: What time?
PUPPET: Check the box. (TEACHER TAKES CARD OUT OF BOX ON STAGE OR ON TABLE NEAR STAGE)
TEACHER: A card with a poem on it!
PUPPET: That is correct. May I have the pleasure of reading it?
TEACHER: Sure, go ahead. (HOLDS CARD SO PUPPET CAN "READ")
PUPPET: It's time to sing a song of cheer
Because we have some new ones here.
TEACHER: Thank you for reminding me; I almost forgot.
PUPPET: Look in the box again.
TEACHER: Is there another card in there?
PUPPET: Look and see.
TEACHER: (TAKING WELCOME BUTTONS OUT OF BOX) Well, how about this! You put the welcome buttons in the box too. Good for you.
PUPPET: (LEADS WELCOME SONG AND GIVES BUTTONS—OR SUPERVISES THE GIVING OF BUTTONS)

PUPPET WITH A "NOISE" PROBLEM

Puppeteer has a bicycle horn, squeak toy, duck whistle, or kazoo in one hand and operates the puppet with the other.

PUPPET: (ENTERS; LOOKS AROUND; OPENS MOUTH AS PUPPETEER HONKS HORN) Oh, oh!
TEACHER: Here you are fooling around and you're supposed to do the welcomes today.
PUPPET: I'm ready. . .I think. (CLEARS THROAT) Today I (honk). (SCANS AUDIENCE; CLEARS THROAT) Today I want to (honk). . . Today (honk).
TEACHER: You did it again!
PUPPET: Did what?
ACHER: Swallowed a bicycle horn. (PUPPET NODS HEAD SLOWLY) Try real hard to make that horn behave and get about your business.
PUPPET: (NODS HEAD VIGOROUSLY) O.K. (CLEARS THROAT TWICE. SPEAKING FASTER) Today it is my great joy and privilege to welcome all you visitors. (PUPPET WELCOMES VISITORS WITH NO PROBLEM) And now it's time for me to say, good (honk). . . good (honk). You all come back next (honk). . .next (honk). I give up. Goodbye.

NOTE: PUPPET #2 can take the place of the TEACHER. Only one puppeteer is needed if the noisemaker is taped to a harmonica holder; thus the puppeteer can bite the bulb of a horn, bite a squeak toy, or hum into a kazoo without needing the use of a hand.

(Music stores carry kazoos and harmonica holders.)

Friend Puppet Celebrates Birthdays

A puppet can participate in all or part of whatever procedure you use for celebrating birthdays. You might like to try the following ideas.

THE BIRTHDAY SONG

Most children will be delighted if a puppet sings the birthday song to him. However, some children may be disappointed if the whole group doesn't also sing to them. Therefore, after the puppet sings, have the group repeat the song, or sing a second verse, either with or without the puppet.

KISS, HUG, PAT ON HEAD, OR HANDSHAKE

Young children usually enjoy receiving a birthday kiss, hug, pat on the head or handshake; let each child choose which action he prefers (from those your puppet is capable of performing).

YOU FORGOT

The teacher has skipped the birthdays and started whatever comes next.

PUPPET: Oh, no!

TEACHER: What's wrong?

PUPPET: I'm not sure, but something's wrong. I was supposed to make sure you didn't forget something today, and I think you forgot whatever it was that I was supposed to remind you of. (TO GROUP) Can you think of anything we've forgotten to do this morning? (BIRTHDAYS) Thanks kids, we wouldn't want to forget anything that important.

HIDE AND GO LOOK

TEACHER: Argyle was supposed to have the box of birthday buttons on the table before Sunday School today, but I guess he forgot. Let's call him. (TEACHER LOOKS AT ONE SIDE OF STAGE AS CHILDREN CALL. ARGYLE POPS UP AND DOWN AT OPPOSITE END—OR LOOKS AWAY FROM STAGE WHEN CHILDREN CALL. ON FOURTH CALL, ARGYLE IS FOUND.) So there you are! The birthday button box isn't on the table.

ARGYLE: I know. . .I thought we could play *Hide and Go Look* this morning.
TEACHER: How do we play *Hide and Go Look*?
ARGYLE: I've already done the first part; I already hidded the button box.
TEACHER: You mean you already hid the box?
ARGYLE: That's what I said. . .I already hidded the box. Now somebody is supposed
              to go look. I'll give you a hint. . .the box is someplace that sounds like *taste*.
              (TEACHER GUIDES CHILDREN TO THINK OF WASTE BASKET
              AND HAS CHILD FIND BOX)

IT'S MY TURN

PUPPET: (AFTER BIRTHDAY TIME IS ANNOUNCED) It's turn, it's turn. (RING
              CALL BELL OR BLOW HORN) It's turn! (GIGGLE)
TEACHER: What do you mean, it's turn, it's turn?
PUPPET: It's my turn to do the birthdays this week.
TEACHER: O.K., it's fun to take turns. (PUPPET CONDUCTS PROCEDURE)

   NOTE: Turn can be between puppet and teacher or between two or more puppets.
(Call bells are available at stationery stores.)

HAPPY BIRTHDAY TO ME!

PUPPET: (BOUNCING AND SINGING) Happy birthday to me, Happy birthday to
              me, Happy birthday dear me, Happy birthday to me.
TEACHER: Wait a minute, are you singing the birthday song to yourself again?
PUPPET: Well, somebody said it was birthday time and I didn't know who to sing to
              so I sang to me; but I'd rather sing to somebody else. . .Who had a birthday
              this past week?
TEACHER: Whoa. . .wait a minute. You can't do the birthdays without the button box,
              and it's not on the table.
PUPPET: That's because the box is in here with me. O.K., now, who had a birthday?
              (AFTER SONG, PUPPET HANDS OUT BUTTONS, USING HANDS
              OR MOUTH—OR RAISES STICK WITH BUTTON(S) TAPED TO
              IT)

I'LL HELP HIM

ADLEY: (ENTERS AFTER BIRTHDAYS
              HAVE BEEN RECOGNIZED.
              SPEAKS FAST IN NONSENSE
              SYLLABLES) Babbledabtopdeed-
              lediddle. . .
TEACHER: Oh, no, that's Adley. He's talking
              FAST AGAIN. I wish he'd learn
              to speak right all the time. Just
              when we think he's learned, he
              starts talking lickety-split again,
              and then nobody can understand
              him.
HESTIRA: Mrs. Jones, I know what he said.
TEACHER: Please tell us, Hestira.
HESTIRA: He said he wanted to do the
              birthdays next week.

TEACHER:	(TO ADLEY) I'd love to have you do the birthdays next week, Adley, but I'm afraid you'll talk so fast no one would understand you.
HESTIRA:	I'll work with Adley all week. If he can say some words slowly next week, will you let him help the week after that?
TEACHER:	Well, yes, Hestira, but it seems like an impossible task.
ADLEY:	Babbledabtopdeedlediddle. . .
TEACHER:	Hestira sure has a job cut out for her next week.

(NEXT WEEK)

HESTIRA:	Last week you said if Adley could say some words slowly this week, he could help with the birthdays next week. Did you forget?
TEACHER:	Oh, I'm very sorry, I did forget. Will you ever forgive me, Adley?
ADLEY:	(VERY SLOWLY) Yes.
TEACHER:	I don't believe it. I actually understood you. Can you say anything else?
ADLEY:	(SLOWLY) Hap. . .py. . .birth. . .day. . .Hap. . .py. . .birth. . .day.
TEACHER:	I'm so proud of you. Next week you can do the birthdays.
ADLEY:	(RAPIDLY) I'm so happy I can't wait until next week. Babbledabtopdeedlediddle. . .
TEACHER:	Poor Adley, he's going to have to practice a lot this week.

(Next week Adley does the birthdays slowly, forgetting only once or twice, but slows down when reminded.)

Friend Puppet Helps with Offerings

Puppets are a valuable aid to (1) encourage sacrificial cheerful giving, (2) motivate and (3) help children understand the purpose for giving.

If the issue arises, a puppet who gives money does it just to join in, to help, or so people will be happy. A puppet should not give so that God will be pleased with him, because a puppet is not a person capable of a relationship with God. However, if a puppet represents a real person in a Christian story dramatization, he may give to please God, because then it is not the puppet, but the person he is representing, who has the relationship with God.

INCREASE DELIGHT IN GIVING

Hold a puppet near the offering basket as children give their money. Have the puppet make comments to the teacher and the children regarding the joy of giving and what the money will be used for.

TO OVERCOME SELFISHNESS AND TEACH CHEERFUL GIVING

FIRST SKIT: Negative Example

PUPPET   I have ten pennies and they're all mine. To give may be fine but boy, will I whine! I'm going to give one of my pennies, but it's going to hurt something awful. I'll go get my penny now. Bobby, will you get something* for me to drop it into? (PUPPET EXITS. BOBBY HOLDS PAN. PUPPET ENTERS WITH PENNY IN HANDS OR MOUTH, DROPS PENNY, MAKES NOISE AS IF IN PAIN) Oh. . . ow . . .See, I told you it would hurt. . .oh. . .ow (EXITS WITH EXAGGERATED GROANS)

SECOND SKIT: Positive Example

PUPPET: (CHEERFULLY) Is it offering time? I have ten pennies and I'm going to put one in the offering. I'll go get my penny. Bobby, will you hold the pan? (PUPPET EXITS: BOBBY HOLDS PAN: PUPPET ENTERS AND DROPS PENNY.) It is fun to give. . .I just knew it would be. Wait a minute, I'm going to get another penny. (EXITS; ENTERS; DROPS PENNY.) 'Bye now. (EXITS SINGING)

*Offering basket, cake pan or wide tin can. (Penny will make noise when dropped in metal pan. Do not use pie pan as penny may slide out.)

BIBLE VERSE: God loves a cheerful giver. II Corinthians 9:7.

EMPHASIZE A SPECIAL PROJECT OFFERING

TEACHER: I can't find the offering baskets. Do you boys and girls have any idea where they might be? I think we'd better call Snappy. (SNAPPY ENTERS AFTER THIRD CALL) Snappy, have you seen our offering baskets?

SNAPPY: Well. . .maybe.

TEACHER: Snappy, do you have the offering baskets?

SNAPPY: Well. . .yes.

TEACHER: Don't you know it's time to take the offering?

SNAPPY: That's why I took the baskets.

TEACHER: I don't understand.

SNAPPY: Well, I wanted to make sure I had the chance to remind the boys and girls that every Sunday this month we're taking a special offering for the missionaries' children so we can send them some Christmas presents. I just wanted to make sure everybody knew that.

TEACHER: That's right, Snappy. Thank you for reminding us. Now may we have the baskets?

SNAPPY: Sure, tell someone to come up, and I'll hand them over.

INCREASE UNDERSTANDING OF THE PURPOSE FOR PROJECT OFFERING

Example: If several offerings will be taken for the purchase of books for a Christian school in Alaska, dress a puppet in Eskimo costume and give him a name like Mitka. Have Mitka appear over a bookcase (or over a box placed on top of a book-case) and briefly explain the need for books.

After each offering is taken and counted, write the amount on a paper fish that has a paper clip attached. Place the fish in a fishbowl or box.

At an appropriate time, have Mitka appear and *go fishing,* using a stick with a string and magnet attached. (It may help to sew the stick to Mitka's hand and tuck the end under his arm.)

To represent books that will be purchased, add books (any books) to the bookcase according to the amount of offering. Have Mitka express great delight over each new book.

NOTE: A new book could be added for each $1.00 of offering if it is explained to the children that each book represents $1.00 and not an actual book.

THE SACRIFICIAL OFFERING

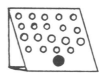

PROPS. Tape 19 dimes and 1 nickel to cardboard. Use real money or pieces of cardboard covered with foil.

For stage with stageboard (shelf): fold cardboard as in first drawing.

For hand-held prop: glue handle to back of prop (second drawing). Handle can be several layers of cardboard glued together.
For handle prop to rest unattended over narrow stage: glue cardboard "spacer" between handle and cardboard holding money.

Puppets: Name any boy puppets "Charlie" and "Sam."

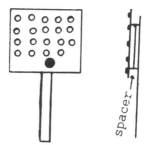

CHARLIE: (LOOKING AT MONEY) 1. . .2. . .3. . .4. . .
SAM: (ENTERS) Hi, Charlie.
CHARLIE: (LOOKS AT SAM) Hi, cousin. (LOOKS AT MONEY) 1. . .2. . .3. . .(LOOKS AT SAM) I'm sure glad you could visit us for the weekend. (LOOKS AT MONEY) 1. . .2. . .3. . .4. . .5. . .
SAM: Say, that's a lot of dimes you have there! How many do you have?
CHARLIE: That's what I'm trying to find out. You want to listen while I count?
SAM: Sure.
CHARLIE: 1. . .2. . .3. . .4 . . .5. . .6. . .7. . .8. . .9 . . .10 . . .11. . .12. . .13. . .14. . .15. . .16. . . 17 (SLOWLY AND EXCITEDLY) . . .18. . .19. . .WOW! I have enough!
SAM: Enough for what?
CHARLIE: For a Super-Duper-Blue-Blooper Racer!
SAM: That's great! (HESITATES) Uh, but Charlie, I thought you already had a Super-Blue-Blooper Racer.
CHARLIE: I do have a Super-Blue-Blooper Racer. Now I want a Super-Duper-Blue-Blooper racer.
SAM: Oh, I see. . .What's the nickel for?
CHARLIE: That's to put in the (STUMBLES OVER WORD) sac-ri-fi-cial offering in Sunday School for some missionaries that need more equipment for their hospital in Africa.
SAM: Sac-ri-fi-cial. . .What does sacrificial mean?
CHARLIE: It means when you give up something so you can give to others.
SAM: Oh. (LOOKING AT DIMES, SPEAKING SLOWLY AND THOUGHT-FULLY) Nineteen dimes for a Super-Duper-Blue-Blooper Racer.
CHARLIE: (LOOKING AT NICKLE, SPEAKING SLOWLY AND THOUGHT-FULLY) One nickel for the offering. . .hm-m-m-m. . . (AFTER A MOMENT's SILENCE) Sam. . .
SAM: Yes, Charlie?
CHARLIE: I really want a Super-Duper-Blue-Blooper Racer.
SAM: I'm sure you do.
CHARLIE: But that missionary hospital needs equipment, and they need it NOW!
SAM: That's right.
CHARLIE: (LOOKING AT MONEY) Listen to me, dimes, and you too, nickel, tomorrow is Sunday. When tomorrow gets here I'm going to put you where you'll do the most good—right in the offering basket.
SAM: Charlie, I brought some extra spending money with me. Would it be O.K. if I put it in the offering tomorrow?
CHARLIE: Terrific idea. Let's get our money ready to go.
SAM: I'll help you unstick yours from the cardboard. (AFTER A SLIGHT PAUSE) Charlie, do you feel good inside?
CHARLIE: I sure do.
SAM: (AS CHARLIE, SAM, AND MONEY EXIT) Me-e-e-e too.

Friend Puppet Prepares Group for Prayer

A puppet can prepare a group for prayer, but a person should be in charge of a time of worship. A puppet should refer to those worshiping as *you*, never as *we*. The only time a puppet should pray is when he is taking part in a Christian story dramatization, for then it is not the puppet, but the person he is representing, who has the relationship with God.

To prepare a group for prayer a puppet can: announce prayer time; talk about subjects for prayer; be delighted that children have the privilege of prayer; develop appreciation for the privilege of prayer and encourage an attitude of reverence.

A QUIET PRAYER TIME

One group of four-year-olds had each been given a puppet to use during song time and memory verse time. The teachers wondered what should be done with the puppets during prayer time. They decided to ask the children not to touch the puppets after placing them in their laps and to hold very still so the puppets wouldn't make any noise. The result was "an amazingly quiet prayer time."

Note: In situations other than the above, it is best to have puppets out of sight during prayer—so children won't be tempted to look at them.

WHERE'S SAM?

PUPPET: (LOOKING AROUND FOR A CERTAIN CHILD) I don't see Sam here today.

TEACHER: Sam isn't here because he's sick.

PUPPET: Boys and girls, do you think God would want you to pray for Sam? Why don't you do that right now. I'll go in my puppet house while you pray. (IF CHILDREN OBJECT TO PUPPET LEAVING) That's where puppets go when people pray. 'Bye.

GOD IS ALWAYS READY TO LISTEN

#1: Do you know what I learned last week?

#2: No, what?

#1: I learned that a lady in Japan went to the temple of her god and rang a bell.

#2: Why did she ring a bell?

#1: Because she thought her god might be asleep. She wanted to be sure he was awake when she prayed, so she rang a bell.

#2: Do these boys and girls have a bell to ring?

#1: They don't need one!

#2: Why not?

#1: Because they pray to the one true God. The lady in Japan prayed to a false god. The Christian's God is the only real God, and He never sleeps. He's always ready to listen to the prayers of His children. Isn't that wonderful?

#2: It sure is. Say, It's almost prayer time. Let's go down and be real quiet while these boys and girls pray. . .shhh.

Friend Puppets Help Give Announcements

Puppets will help liven up announcement time, and you will find that retention of announcements is markedly increased when they are given by puppets in an interesting fashion. After such an announcement it's doubtful if anyone will be able to say, "Oh, I didn't hear about that." Even the teacher of an adult class remarked, "If I especially want my class to remember an announcement, I do it with puppets."

If you have several puppets, all can be used to make announcements. Occasionally two might fuss over who gets to do it that day ("fun-type" fussing, with happy solution). When announcing events, if appropriate, have puppets comment, "That sounds like fun."

The announcements are given here as samples and, of course, you will need to adapt them to fit your needs. They contain information that is generally classified as an announcement. However, keep in mind that information such as:

- the name of the next song;
- the reference or first word of the current memory verse;
- the names of the main characters in the Bible story;
- the name of the next song;
- that it's time for dismissal; etc.

can also be treated in the same way. If there are no regular announcements, it would add interest to a session to give one of the above bits of information in the framework of an announcement.

ANNOUNCEMENT SIGN

To signal the beginning of announcements, you may wish to raise a sign in a puppet theater and then lower it. At the same time a voice offstage, or a puppet onstage could say, "Time for announcements." Even if announcements are then given in a conventional manner, they are more likely to be remembered because attention has been drawn to them.

To Make Sign: Cover piece of corrugated cardboard with decorative paper. Glue ruler or yardstick to back of cardboard. Cover stick with felt or other covering. Print "ANNOUNCE-MENT" on separate piece of paper and pin paper to sign. Or attach "ANNOUNCEMENT" sign to large grocery bag (folded flat). Bag can be held in puppeteer's hand, or by yardstick placed inside bag. To hold stick in position, staple bag together at sides of stick near top of bag.

ANNOUNCEMENT SONG

A routine for announcement time could be to have the group sing "The Announcement Song." One or more puppets would respond to the call of the song.

A – nounce-ments, a – nounce-ments, a – nou-ounce ments.

The signal for the song to be sung could be the raising of the announcement sign. Or, if there is just one puppet fussy enough to require the song before he appears, a separate sign saying "Song, Please" could be raised as a signal for the group to sing the song.

Rather than have the group sing, the song could be played on the piano or played on a kazoo. A kazoo could be played by the unseen puppeteer or by a puppet on stage. (Puppeteer plays kazoo, as a puppet with kazoo in mouth or fastened to hand, pretends to play.)

PUPPET #1:   (CLEARS THROAT) Attention please, everyone. Argyle says he has an announcement to give.
ARGYLE: (ENTERS AND WHISPERS SILENTLY IN PUPPET #1'S EAR. EXITS)
PUPPET #1:   Argyle says he won't give the announcement until he hears the Announcement Song. I'll humor him and sing it. (SINGS ANNOUNCE-MENT SONG)
ARGYLE: (ENTERS AND WHISPERS IN #1'S EAR. EXITS)
PUPPET #1:   He wants to hear you kids sing the song. I'll count to three, then you sing, O.K? One. . .two. . .three. (CHILDREN SING. #1 CAN LEAD SONG)
ARGYLE: (ENTERS) Oh, I just love to hear kids sing that song. Now, the announcement I want to make is. . .

WHERE IS EVERYBODY?

TEACHER: It's announcement time, so let's sing "The Announcement Song." Farley always insists that we sing him this song before he'll appear, you know. (GROUP SINGS)
FARLEY: (ENTERS, FACING LEFT) Yes, yes, I heard the song, and here I am, but who am I supposed to give the announcement to? There's nobody here. Maybe I dreamed I heard the song. (EXITS)
TEACHER: Looks like Farley is having trouble finding us. Let's sing the song again. (GROUP SINGS)
FARLEY: (ENTERS FACING RIGHT) I know I heard The Announcement Song, and that's my cue to come and make an announcement. . .and it's a very interesting announcement I have today. Too bad nobody's here. (EXITS)
TEACHER: Let's try singing one more time. (GROUP SINGS)
FARLEY: (ENTERS WITH BACK TO AUDIENCE) Something is definitely wrong. I could give the announcement but nobody would hear it. I'll just go back where I came from. (EXITS)
TEACHER: I'll tell you what. . .This week I'll give Farley lessons on how to find people. You all come back next week and see if he can find us. I sure hope we'll all get to hear the announcement next week. . .I wonder what it is!

LISTEN REAL GOOD

#1: I'm going to tell you something. Listen real good now, O.K?

#2: O.K.

#1: There's going to be a special film here at church next Sunday at 7 o'clock. Now tell me what I said.

#2: There's going to be a sewing circle just for ladies at Mrs. Johnson's house tomorrow. . .How'd I do?

#1: Not so good! Let's try again. . .slower this time. (SLOWLY) There's going to be a special film here at church next Sunday at 7 o'clock.

#2: What kind of a film?

#1: It's about the adventures of a Christian boy in Africa.

#2: Sounds good. Why is it going to be at church?

#1: Because that's the best place to have it!

#2: Why is it going to be at 7 o'clock?

#1: Because that's the best time to have it! Can you say it right this time? Try it.

#2: (SLOWLY) There's going to be a special film here at church next Sunday at 7 o'clock. Now tell me what I said.

#1: There's going to be a special film here at church next Sunday at 7 o'clock. . .What'd I say that for?. . .You're the one. . .You're impossible! (#1 FAINTS)

#2: (LOOKS AROUND; EXITS; RE-ENTERS) You all be sure and come. You'll be glad you did.

I FOUND A NOTE

PROP: Announcement paper pinned to signboard.
(SUNDAY SCHOOL SUPERINTENDENT IS IN ROOM, BUT OUT OF SIGHT)

PUPPET: (ENTERS LOOKING EVERYWHERE BUT AT GROUP, THEN LOOKS AT GROUP) Oh, there you are. I've been looking all over for you *because* I get to read you a note today. Mr. Jones has a habit of leaving notes in different places. If I find one, I'm supposed to read it to you. I'll go get the note. (EXITS, RE-ENTERS WITH NOTE PINNED TO SIGNBOARD) You'll like this note. (MR. JONES COMES INTO VIEW) Just wait 'til you hear it! (READING IN LOUD VOICE, SLOWLY) Let's have a. . .

SUP'T: (INTERRUPTING) Say, Mr. Puppet. . .

PUPPET: Sir, my name is Booker.

SUP'T: O.K., Booker, what are you reading?

PUPPET: A note I found, just like you told me to do.

SUP'T: I don't remember any note. Well, O.K, go ahead and read it.

PUPPET: (READING) Let's have a surprise. . .

SUP'T: I don't remember anything about a surprise. . .Well. . .O.K. . .read on.

PUPPET: (READING) Let's have a surprise next Sunday for everyone who comes to Sunday. . .

SUP'T:	(INTERRUPTING, ALARMED) Wait. . .WAIT. . .Now I remember. That's not a note for the boys and girls; that's a note for the teachers!
PUPPET:	It doesn't say so. I'm sorry if I blabbed your surprise secret all over to everybody.
SUP'T:	That's O.K. It's not your fault. You just did what I told you to do. Say, where did you find that note?
PUPPET:	In your Sunday School quarterly. That's a really great book.
SUP'T:	That's because it has Bible verses and Bible stories in it. The Bible is different from any book in the world. It's a letter to people from God.
PUPPET:	You mean the God who made all the animals and all the people and everything?
SUP'T:	That's right.
PUPPET:	I've got to hurry and find that book and read some more. 'Bye. (STARTS TO EXIT)
SUP'T:	Hey, come back here. What are we going to do about you reading that note to everybody? Say, maybe they didn't hear what you said. Boys and girls, did you hear what Booker said? (GROUP RESPONDS)
PUPPET:	Mr. Jones, I don't think there's any problem.
SUP'T:	Why not?
PUPPET:	Well, now that the boys and girls know about the surprise, they'll try extra hard to be here and maybe they'll get some absentees to come back.
SUP'T:	And maybe they'll invite some new people to come.
PUPPET:	Yeah, that'd be great. . .especially because everyone who comes will learn about God.
SUP'T:	Booker, I must say, you're very smart.
PUPPET:	Mr. Jones, will I get a surprise if I come next Sunday?
SUP'T:	Of course.
PUPPET:	If I bring a friend, will he get a surprise too?
SUP'T:	He sure will.
PUPPET:	I'll be here for sure and I'll try my best to bring a friend. In the meantime, I'm going to be reading in that Sunday School quarterly. 'Bye, everybody. See you all next Sunday.

NOTE: The surprise might be Scripture balloons or Bible verse pencils, perhaps with peanuts tied in plastic wrap and attached. Make sure Booker returns the following Sunday with a new friend, and that they both get their "surprises."

For other announcements, that are supposed to be read, the puppet could find the notes in odd places such as the refrigerator, waste basket, a sandwich or under a rug.

I FOUND A SIGNCARD. . .AND ANOTHER. . .AND ANOTHER

PROPS: Signcards, made of folded paper or cardboard, saying: 7:30; church; Friday; dinner (whatever you wish to announce). Write the words on the back of the cards also so the puppeteer can read them for rearranging.

SETTING FOR SKIT: Skit is to be performed during song time.

PUPPET: (POPS UP AFTER SONG) Look what I found. (FOLDED SIGNCARD IS PLACED OVER EDGE OF STAGE) What does the signcard say? (GROUP READS CARD) *7:30!*. . .That doesn't tell

us much. Maybe I can find another card. I'll go look while you sing another song. (EXITS, RE-ENTERS AFTER SONG AND PLACES CARD OVER STAGE) What does this card say? (GROUP READS CARD) Now we have *7:30* and *church*, but I think there must be at least one more card. Sing another song, O.K? (EXITS, RE-ENTERS AFTER SONG AND PLACES 3RD CARD OVER STAGE) What does this one say? (GROUP READS) Oh boy, it looks like something is happening here at church at 7:30 Friday. I wonder what? Sing another song. (EXITS, RE-ENTERS AFTER SONG) I found another signcard. You want to see it? (EXITS, RE-ENTERS AND PLACES 4TH CARD OVER STAGE) This card smells like food, yum, yum! What's it say? (GROUP READS) I thought so, yum, yum! Church dinners are such fun! Everybody close your eyes for a minute. (PUPPET REARRANGES CARDS) Open your eyes. Now everybody read the cards. (GROUP READS) Do you like the cards arranged this way better? (PUPPET REARRANGES CARDS IF GROUP PREFERS FIRST ORDER. PUPPET SPEAKS TO ADULT LEADER) Say, Mr. Jones, this church dinner at 7:30 Friday sounds like great fun. Can all these kids come if they can get their parents to bring them?

NOTE: For other announcements of this type, you may wish to bring up signcards in an order that doesn't make sense, perhaps with part of a word on one card and part on another and the two parts mixed in with other words. The puppet could rearrange the cards or he could ask a child to help.

IT'S UPSIDE DOWN!

PROP: Paper, with announcement written on it, pinned to signboard. To make signboard: cover a square piece of corrugated cardboard with decorative paper and glue a cardboard handle at the center of the uncovered side.

PUPPET: Hello to all you boys and girls out there. I have an announcement for you. The announcement is. . .(LOOKS ALL AROUND) Oops, it's not here. Well, I can fix that. (POMPOUSLY) Enter announcement. (SINGS FANFARE) Dah-dah-dah-dah. . .dah-dah! (SIGN-BOARD ENTERS UPSIDE DOWN) Now I'm ready. The announcement is (LOOKS AT SIGNBOARD AND SAYS NON-SENSE SYLLABLES) I didn't know I could speak a foreign language. Hm-m-m-m, maybe that's not a foreign language. . .What do you think?. . .You think maybe the sign is upside down? What should I do?. . .Turn it right sideup?. . .I'll see if I can. (PRETENDS  TO TURN SIGNBOARD WITH MOUTH OR HANDS AS PUPPETEER TURNS IT) Aha! Now the words make sense. (READS ANNOUNCEMENT)

WHO'S THAT SNEEZING?
(Script can be adapted for countries other than Brazil.)

PROPS: Banana in paper bag. Puppet has loose-fitting hat, or men's handkerchief knotted to make hat. To make hat: Lay hanky flat; fold two ends to center and sew or pin these ends together. Tie knot in each end not folded to center. (Placement of knots will depend on size of puppet's head.)

TEACHER: For our last song (PEDRO SNEEZES OFFSTAGE) let's sing. . .Did I hear somebody sneeze? Did you hear somebody sneeze? (LOOKS ALL AROUND)

PEDRO:* (ENTERS, SNEEZES) Eeet's me (SNEEZES) Oh, these sneezes are such a problem. (SNEEZES, LOWERING HEAD OR JUMPING 'TIL HAT FALLS OFF) See, I even sneezed my hat off! Eeef I just had a bananaba I think I could stop sneezing. (SIGHING) A-h-h-h, I love bananabas. (SNEEZES) Anyone here got a bananaba I could have? (SNEEZES)

TEACHER: Who are you and what are you doing here?

PEDRO: O meu nome e' Pedro,** My name is Pedro and I am from Brazil. Brazil is a country in South America. People speak Portuguese in Brazil, you know.

TEACHER: Is that why you say *bananaba* for *banana*?

PEDRO: No, that's just a word I have trouble with sometimes. Doesn't anybody (SNEEZES) have a bananaba? (TEACHER TAKES BANANA FROM PAPER BAG) Ala', a bananaba!

TEACHER: Brazil grows lots of bananas so I brought one with me today to remind me to tell the boys and girls about Mr. and Mrs. Johnson.

PEDRO: I know Mr. and Mrs. Johnson. They're missionaries to my country, Brazil.

TEACHER: Yes, and they are going to be here with us for our missionary conference this week.

PEDRO: Say, now that you've remembered to tell the boys and girls about the Johnsons, could I have that (SNEEZES) bananaba?

TEACHER: Sure. (PUTS BANANA IN PUPPET THEATER)

PEDRO: Obrigadu. . .Thank you. . .thank you very much.

TEACHER: Pedro, are you coming to our missionary conference this week?

PEDRO: (ENTHUSIASTICALLY TO TEACHER) Sim, sim! Wild horses couldn't keep me away! (ENTHUSIASTICALLY TO GROUP) Yes, yes! Wild horses couldn't keep me away! Adeus. (SNEEZES) I'd better go eat my bananaba. 'Bye.

*Any puppet can be used for Pedro if explanation is made. Before the songs, have the puppet say, "For a puppet skit later today we need a Portuguese puppet, but we don't have any; so I'm going to pretend I'm Pedro from Portugal. See 'ya later." If possible, add an accessory—in addition to the hat—to make the puppet look Portuguese.

**Pronunciations.
My name is Peter: O meu nome e' Pedro (o mew nohm a Pay'dro—both *a*'s as in *ate*)
Greeting: Ala' (ah lah')
Thank you: Obrigadu (o bree gah' dew—*bree* as in *breeze*)
Yes: Sim (seem)
Goodbye: Adeus (ah day' oos—*oos* as in *moose*)

PLEASE KEEP YOUR MOUTH CLOSED

Puppets must be able to hold a piece of paper in their mouth.

PROP: 8-1/2" x 11" paper with large scribbles on it

#1:   You know what?

#2:   No, what?

#1:   You know what I'd like to hear right now?

#2:   No, what?

#1:   I'd like to hear an announcement.

#2:   What kind of an announcement?

#1:   I don't know. . .a good announcement of some kind.

#2:   Wouldn't you rather hear me sing a song? I'm a good song singer.

#1:   Nope, I'd like to hear an announcement. Go down to your announcement file and get me one, O.K?

#2:   Oh, all right, if you insist. (MUMBLES AS EXITS) I'd sure rather sing a song. ENTERS WITH PAPER IN MOUTH) M-m-m-m-m-m. (NUDGES #1) M-M-M-M-M-M!

#1:   (TO GROUP) I wonder what he wants me to do. . .Do you think he wants me to take the announcement paper in my mouth and hold it so he can read it?

#2:   (NODDING HEAD VIGOROUSLY) M-M-M-M-M! (#1 TAKES PAPER) Well. . . finally. Now I can read this. It says a missionary is coming. . .

#1:   (OPENS MOUTH WIDE, SPEAKS EXCITEDLY AS PAPER DROPS TO FLOOR) Where? Is the missionary coming to our church?

#2:   Look what you did. . .you lost the announcement. I can't read it if you don't hold it!

#1:   (LOOKS AT ANNOUNCEMENT ON FLOOR) Oh, oh! Jane, will you hand me the announcement please? Don't try to read it; it's written in puppet language. (JANE HANDS PAPER TO PUPPET) M-m-m-m.

#2:   (TO JANE) She's saying, "Thank you." (TO #1) Will you please keep your mouth closed! (READING) Let's see. . .Yes, a missionary is coming to our church. . .

#1:   (OPENS MOUTH WIDE, SPEAKS EXCITEDLY AS PAPER DROPS) When?. . . when is the missionary coming? (LOOKS AT PAPER ON FLOOR) Oops. . .Jane, I need some help again. (JANE HANDS PAPER TO PUPPET) M-m-m-m.

#2:   (TO JANE) She's saying, "Thank you" again. (TO #1) Now, will you PLEASE keep your mouth closed? (READING) Where were we?. . .Oh, yes, a missionary is coming right here to our church next Sunday morning at 11:00.

#1:   (OPENS MOUTH AS BEFORE, SPEAKS SUSPICIOUSLY) Who gets to hear the missionary? If the meeting is only for adults, these kids can't go. (LOOKS AT PAPER) I did it again, huh?. . .Help, Jane. (TO #2) Will you hurry and read to see if kids get to hear the missionary?

#2:   Yes, but you have to hold the paper!

#1:   You're right. (TAKES PAPER FROM JANE) M-m-m-m.

#2:   (READING) The meeting is for everybody.

#1:   (OPENS MOUTH AND DROPS PAPER AS BEFORE—OR DROPS PAPER INSIDE STAGE. SPEAKING SUSPICIOUSLY) Are you sure that's an announcement for our church? Maybe it's an announcement for a church far away from here.

#2:   It's an announcement for our church all right.

#1:   Maybe it's last year's announcement. (TO TEACHER OR SUPERINTENDENT) Mr. Jones, is it really true? Is a real live missionary coming right here to our church?

(IF PAPER WAS DROPPED OUTSIDE STAGE AND JANE HOLDS IT UP,

#1 or #2 THANKS JANE, TAKES PAPER AND DROPS IT BEHIND STAGE.)

I CAN'T SAY THAT WORD

PROP: Paper with announcement written on it. The paper can be held by a second puppet or pinned to a signboard and held by the puppeteer. To make a signboard, glue a stick to a piece of corrugated cardboard. Cardboard may be covered with decorative paper.

PUPPET: Hi, kids, you all listen to this announcement I'm about to read, O.K? (PUPPET WITH ANNOUNCEMENT, OR SIGNBOARD, ENTERS) This announcement says, (READING) "Everybody be sure and come next Sunday, because we're going to have a special surprise visitor from (STUMBLING OVER WORD) Ma. . .Ma. . ." (TO GROUP) I can't say that word. I'll just keep reading. (READING) "The missionary will have many interesting things to tell us about Ma. . .Ma. . .da. . ." (TO GROUP) There's that word again. Does anybody know of a country that starts with Mada? (IF THERE'S NO RESPONSE, PUPPET READS WORD WITH DIFFICULTY) That's it! Madagascar. I'll read the rest. (READS SILENTLY, THEN SPEAKS WITH ALARM) I can't believe my eyes! (EXITS SCREAMING; RE-ENTERS SLOWLY WITH BODY SHAKING; SPEAKS TO AUDIENCE AS IF AFRAID) It says, "The missionary is bringing a snake 12 feet long!" Maybe I'd better read that part again. (READING) "The missionary is bringing a snake *skin* 12 feet long." Whew, what a relief! Wait a minute. . .maybe there'll be a snake in the snake skin. Oh, I hope not. (EXITS SAYING) I sure do hope not. . .hope not. . .not. . .not.

NOTE: For other similar announcement skits, a word could be smeared or left out. After the puppet comments on the problem, the script would go as follows:

PUPPET: I wonder who wrote this announcement. Excuse me just a minute, please. (EXITS; PAUSES; Re-ENTERS) The character that wrote this announcement says the word in question is (ENTHUSIASTICALLY) *contest* (whatever word is in question). (OR THE PUPPET MIGHT SAY, "I can't find anybody that knows about this announcement, but I think I can find out before Sunday School is over.") (EXITS; RE-ENTERS LATER IN SESSION).

I CAN'T SING

A party was announced the previous week.

#1:   (SOFT, THEN EXAGGERATED, FUN-TYPE CRYING) Waa. . .boo-hoo-hoo. . .WAA. . .BOO-HOO-HOO. . .W-A-A. . .
#2:   What's the matter with you?
#1:   (DISTRESSED) I'm supposed to sing a song at the party that's going to be next Saturday at 1:30 right here in this room, and I can't sing it! (CRIES)
#2:   Why not?
#1:   (DISTRESSED) Because I lost the words. I put them someplace special until I was

ready to learn them, and now I can't find them. (CRIES)

#2: What's the name of the song? (#1 WHISPERS IN #2'S EAR, CRIES) Stop that silly crying.

#1: (EXCITEDLY) Do you know the words?

#2: Yep.

#1: (TO AUDIENCE) Hey, you all come and hear me sing that song Saturday at 1:30 right here in this room.

#2: (CLEARING THROAT) A-hem. . .a-hem. . .AHEM.

#1: Oops. . .I mean you all come and hear US sing. . .party starts at 1:30.

DON'T FORGET THE ANNOUNCEMENT

Toward the end of a song (not a serious-type), puppet appears with paper in his mouth. Tries to get song leader's attention by walking back and forth, jumping up and down, banging his head on the stage, etc. Song leader pays no attention, but by time the song is concluded, children will be notifying the song leader. When alerted, he asks a child to take the paper and bring it to him.

PUPPET: (EXHAUSTED) I didn't know if I'd get through to you today! Thanks, kids, for your help. I was told to deliver this paper to you. . .What a job! (PUPPET FAINTS, FALLING BACKWARD OFF STAGE; THEN ENTERS AND SPEAKS WEAKLY) Don't forget to read it. . .it's an important announcement. . .a-h-h-h. (FAINTS)

WAIT UNTIL NEXT WEEK

Substitute the name of your puppet, superintendent and staff for those in the script.

ROSCOE: (VERY EXCITED, MOVING TO AND FRO) Mrs. Brown, Mr. Nelson! Come here! Miss Wilson, Mr. Scott! (SUPERINTENDENT AND STAFF COME RUNNING UP TO THE PUPPET THEATER)

SUP'T: Roscoe, what's wrong? What's all this about?

ROSCOE: Nothing's wrong! Everything's great! I have the most exciting announcement. (LOOKS AT GROUP) Wait 'til you hear!

SUP'T: Wonderful, Roscoe. Would you like to tell us what your special news is?

ROSCOE: Well. . .(LOOKS EACH WAY TO SEE IF ANYONE IS COMING, AS IF HE'S ABOUT TO SHARE A GREAT SECRET) It's a fantastic secret. (SUP'T AND STAFF LOOK AT EACH OTHER IN EXASPERATION)

SUP'T: Yes, but what is it?

ROSCOE: Well. . .No. . .No, I think I'm going to keep it to myself for awhile. I'm not supposed to tell it this week. (SUP'T AND STAFF MOAN)

SUP'T: Roscoe! You've got us all terribly curious now. We want to hear your special news. (TURNS TO GROUP) Don't we, boys and girls?

ROSCOE: Well, I'll tell you what. . .maybe next week.

SUP'T: Oh, no! Do we have to wait a whole week?. . .O.K. But we'll expect you to tell us next week! (STAFF RETURNS TO SEATS)

ONE WEEK LATER: Repeat opening of skit (Roscoe calls up sup't and staff and says he has a great announcement).

SUP'T: Roscoe, we remember last week you said you had something really special to tell us. What is it?

ROSCOE: Actually. . .I'm not supposed to tell 'til next week. (EVERYONE GROANS)

SUP'T: Roscoe! You said you'd tell us this week!

ROSCOE: I said "maybe"!

SUP'T: O.K., I guess you did. But I wish you'd hurry up. Roscoe, do you PROMISE to tell us next week?

ROSCOE: O.K. (STAFF RETURNS TO SEATS)

ONE WEEK LATER: Repeat opening.

SUP'T: Roscoe, we're all here! What is the important announcement?

ROSCOE: Well. . .maybe I'll wait. . .

SUP'T: Roscoe! You promised!

ROSCOE: Maybe I had my fingers crossed so I didn't really promise.

SUP'T: Roscoe, the Bible doesn't say it's O.K. for people to lie if they have their fingers crossed! And you shouldn't pull that trick either.

ROSCOE: You're right. And this IS the week I'm supposed to tell you that. . .(ROSCOE ANNOUNCES SOME BIG EVENT, SUCH AS A TRIP, SPECIAL PROJECT OR THE SUNDAY SCHOOL PICNIC)

PASS IT ON

TEACHER: You want to help me make an anouncement?

PUPPET: Sure.

TEACHER: O.K. I'll tell you something and then you pass it on.

PUPPET: Pass it on?

TEACHER: After I tell something to you, you pass it on to all those ears out there.

PUPPET: O.K. . . .sounds like fun.

TEACHER: Next Sunday. . .

PUPPET: This Sunday. . .

TEACHER: (SHAKING HEAD) No. . .Next Sunday. . .

PUPPET: Next Sunday. . .

TEACHER: . . .everybody. . .

PUPPET: . . .everybody. . .

TEACHER: . . .will meet in the auditorium. . .

PUPPET: . . .will meet

TEACHER: . . .in the auditorium. . .

PUPPET: . . .in the auditorium. . .

TEACHER: . . .for Sunday School. . .

PUPPET: How come?

TEACHER: Don't ask questions; just pass it on.

PUPPET: . . .for Sunday School. . .

TEACHER: . . .to hear a. . .

PUPPET: . . .to hear a. . .

TEACHER: . . .famous basketball. . .
PUPPET: . . .famous basketball? (TEACHER NODS HEAD) . . .famous basket-
              ball. . .
TEACHER: . . .player speak.
PUPPET: . . .player speak.
TEACHER: Now see if you can say it all together.
PUPPET:*   Next Sunday, everybody will meet in the auditorium for Sunday School to
              hear a famous basketball player speak.

*The puppet can say the announcement correctly, perhaps with hesitation, or the puppet
can require prompting by the teacher. Details of the announcement can be given by the
teacher, perhaps after the puppet asks leading questions.

SNORE, SNORE. . .

PROP: Bottle of vitamin pills.

PUPPET: Are you ever going to be glad you came
              to Sunday School today! Just wait until
              you hear what this really great an-
              nouncement is. The announcement is
              . . .Are you ready?. . .The announcement
              is (YAWNS). . .the announcement is
              (YAWNS; LOWERS HEAD GRAD-
              UALLY—OR TURNS BACK TO
              GROUP—AND SNORES)
TEACHER: Oh, oh! It looks like Lockimer has
              gone to sleep! Let's quietly call him
              and see if we can wake him up.
              (GROUP CALLS)
PUPPET: (WAKING UP) M-m-m-m-ah-ah. What was I doing?. . .Sleeping? What
              was I supposed to be doing?. . .Making an announcement? Ah yes, of
              course. Well, this great announcement is. . .ah. . .(LOWERS HEAD—OR
              TURNS BACK—AND SNORES)
TEACHER: What do we do now?. . .I'll tell you what (TAKES VITAMIN PILL OUT
              OF BOTTLE) Here's a vitamin pill. This ought to give him some energy.
              (TEACHER HANDS PILL TO CHILD, ASKS CHILD TO GIVE IT TO
              PUPPET. PUPPET TAKES PILL, THEN DROPS IT.) Oh me, oh my, it
              seems like Lockimer is too tired even to swallow a vitamin pill. I know
              what I'll do. I'll put him to bed at 6 o'clock next Saturday night. Then
              surely he'll be able to stay awake next Sunday morning long enough to give
              us this great announcement. I'm sorry, but it looks as if we'll all have to
              wait until next Sunday to find out what it is.

HOW DID THIS HAPPEN?

PROP: Piece of paper, with large scribbles, attached to
puppet's nose with loop of tape (sticky side out).

PUPPET: I don't know how this happened, but

somehow the announcement paper got
stuck to my nose! Anybody got an idea how I could get this note off my
nose? I'm getting an eyeache trying to read it this close. (CHILD
VOLUNTEERS). . .Good idea. Ron, after you pull the note off, will you
hold it so I can read it?. . .Thanks.

I WISH I COULD (for Vacation Bible School)
(Puppet #1 faces audience, ignoring #2, until script directs otherwise. Puppet #2 faces #1.)

#1: (WISTFULLY) I wish I could do something this summer. . .like make something.
#2: I know where you can make something this summer.
#1: . . .and hear some stories. . .
#2: I know where you can hear some great stories.
#1: . . .and I wish I could play with a bunch of kids. . .
#2: I know where there'll be a bunch of kids.
#1: . . .and I wish I knew where I could go and eat some cookies.
#2: I know where.
#1: . . .and I wish I could learn some new songs. Boy, all that stuff would sure be fun. But I guess that's wishing for too much.
#2: (YELLING) You haven't heard a word I said.
#1: (LOOKING AT #2) Have you been talking? I haven't heard a word you said.
#2: Yes, I know. I've been saying I know where you can do all those things you've been wishing you could do.
#1: (ENTHUSIASTICALLY) You're kidding! Tell me where! Tell me where!
#2: Right here. . .at Vacation Bible School. . .and it starts tomorrow. You be sure and come.
#1: (TO GROUP) Be sure and come, he says. WOW! Nothing could keep me away. Say, do kids get to come too?. . .Great!. . .I hope I'll see all of you at VACATION BIBLE SCHOOL. . .tomorrow at 9 o'clock.
Note: Be sure puppet #1 does come to VBS and take part.

ONLY TEACHERS CAN COME

#1: The announcement for today is that we're going to have a party next Saturday right here in this room from two to four, and only teachers can come.
#2: (CLEARING THROAT) A-hem!. . .A-HEM. . .A-HEM, A-HEM, A-HEM!
#1: Is something wrong?
#2: I think you might be a bit mixed up.
#1: We're having a party, right?
#2: Right.
#1: And it'll be right here in this room, right?
#2: Right.
#1: . . .from two to four, right?
#2: Right.
#1: And only teachers can come. . .Oh, oh, I bet that's the part I mixed up. A party wouldn't be any fun without kids. Of course you kids get to come. Say, can they bring friends?
#2: Sure.
#1: All you kids, be sure and come and bring some friends. . .hey, why don't you surprise the teachers and bring the whole neighborhood? . . .'Bye.

I WENT FOR A WALK

#1: Guess what I did yesterday?

#2: Did you go for another walk?

#1: Yep, I sure did, and it was a long, long, long walk, and you know where I ended up?

#2: I have no idea. . .Where?

#1: At the County Park. . .isn't that where these kids are going on a hike Saturday?

#2: The very same place.

#1: Boy, that's sure a nice park. (DESCRIBES PARK. #1 ADDS FAVORABLE COMMENTS) These kids are in for a fun time.

#2: What did you do after you left the park?

#1: Well, I was walking along and saw this sign that said Happy Hound, so I went in, and did it ever smell good in there!

#2: The *Happy Hound?* That's the place where we're going to eat after the hike.

#1: Do you know what I'd order to eat if I were one of these kids?

#2: No. . .what?

#1: A hot dog. . .with sauerkraut on it. . .and beans on it. . .and spaghetti on top of the sauerkraut and beans. . .and I'd put all that in a bowl and pour 7-Up all over it. . . yum, Yum, YUM!

#2: I don't know about you!

#1: Hey, you kids, don't forget to meet here at 9:30 Saturday morning.

I MISSED IT!

#1: (CRYING WITH EXAGGERATED MODULATION) Wa-a-a, oh-h-h, boo-hoo-hoo-hoo. (HANGS HEAD OVER STAGE, CONTINUES CRYING)

#2: What's the matter?

#1: (SNIFFLING) I missed it! Oh, I missed it!

#2: Missed what?

#1: (SNIFFLING) The singing group that came to our church last night. . .just the most terrific singing group right here in our church, and I forgot all about it. . . exciting, enthusiastic teenagers and I missed it. (CRIES, HANGS HEAD AND CRIES)

#2: You didn't miss it.

#1: Yes I did.

#2: No you didn't! The group didn't sing last night; they're going to sing tonight.

#1: Are you sure? (JUMPING AROUND) Oh, wow! Oh, joy! (CRIES, HANGS HEAD AND CRIES)

#2: Now what's the matter?

#1: (SNIFFLING) I lost my ticket, and probably some of these kids did, too. (TO GROUP) Did any of you lose your ticket?

#2: What ticket?

#1: (SNIFFLING) That piece of paper they handed out last Sunday. (CRIES)

#2: That wasn't a ticket! It just told the time and place so people wouldn't forget.

#1: Well then, where do we get tickets, so they'll let us in?

#2: You don't need a ticket. It's free for everybody!

#1: Hey kids, did you hear that? You don't need a ticket and the group is singing tonight. You all come and bring your friends and your parents and anybody else that can come. (EXITS, SAYING OR SINGING TO ORIGINAL TUNE) Group sings tonight. . .Don't need a ticket. . .Group sings tonight. . .Don't need a ticket. . . Yeah!

CAN YOU GUESS THE ANNOUNCEMENT?. . .HERE'S A CLUE

Children enjoy guessing. A puppet should be anxious for an announcement to be guessed and should praise an individual or a group when an announcement is guessed.

CAUTION: Don't prolong a time of guessing—keep it lively. Have a puppet ask leading questions and give additional clues, hints or information whenever needed.

ACTION CLUE:

PUPPET: I'm supposed to give an announcement, and I've decided to see if you can guess what it is. First you have to guess what I'm doing. (PUPPET PRE-TENDS TO EAT) That's right, I'm eating. Now, what do you suppose eating has to do with the announcement? (PUPPET HAS GROUP GUESS THE EVENT AND PERHAPS THE TIME, ETC.)

PICTURE OR OBJECT CLUE

PUPPET: I'm going to hold up a picture right now, right here, for all to see. (HOLDS UP PICTURE) Purdy picture, huh? The reason for this picture, right here, right now, for all to see, is that it's my announcement. Well, it's sort of my announcement. You have to guess the rest.

Instead of a magazine picture or drawing, the puppet can hold up an object, perhaps pinned or sewed to a cardboard sign. Or the picture or object can be in a box near the theater and puppet may ask a child to take it out and hold it up for all to see.

WORD CLUE

#1: Would you look at this sign!. . .It says *sore feet*. What's a sign like this doing here?
#2: I knew you'd forget.
#1: Forget what?
#2: Forget the announcement.
#1: Ah. . .er. . .uh. . .Don't tell me, let me guess.
#2: I wasn't going to tell you. . .that's what the sign's for . . .to help you guess.

61

#1: I don't have any idea what sore feet have to do with an announcement! Kids, do you have any ideas? (#1 REPEATS GUESSES FROM GROUP TO #2. IF HIKE ISN'T GUESSED, RAISE 2ND SIGN—*beautiful view*. RAISE MORE SIGNS, WITH #2 GIVING HINTS IF NEEDED. #1 PRAISES CHILD, OR GROUP, FOR FIGURING OUT *hike*). I'm in luck you know. If I go, somebody has to carry me. I don't have any feet, hah-hah!

SCRAMBLED LETTERS

MARELLA: Are you ready for this, kids?. . .Next Saturday, we're going to have a. . . a. . .Evadine, don't you have the sign ready yet?

EVADINE: (VOICE OFFSTAGE) Not yet.

MARELLA: Why not?

EVADINE: Because I'm having a little trouble.

MARELLA: Well, hurry up, please. I can't make the announcement without the sign.

EVADINE: (ENTERS AS SIGN ENTERS) Here we are.

MARELLA: Next Saturday, we're going to have a (READING IN UNBELIEF). . . yrapt? Evadine, I think perhaps you hurried a little too fast!

EVADINE: No, I didn't hurry too fast. I scrambled the letters on purpose. I thought it's be fun to see if the kids could unscramble them.

MARELLA: O.K., kids, can anybody figure out what we're going to have next Saturday? (PARTY)

MISSING LETTERS

PUPPET: Something special is happening next Sunday. Here's a sign telling what. . .The only problem is that the sign doesn't make sense. But hold on. . .we have some clues. See those scattered letters? Those are clues. Anybody think they know what the words are? (PUPPET OR TEACHER FILLS IN LETTERS UNTIL WORDS ARE SAID—PROMOTION SUNDAY)

CODED WORD

PUPPET: A few minutes from now, we're going to have a. . .(RAISES SIGN) Who'll be the first to figure out what we're going to have. Look at the alphabet code chart for the letters in the word. (VISITOR)

Chart:
$$\frac{\text{a b c d e f g h i j k l . . . . z}}{\text{1 2 3 4 5 6 7 8 9 10 11 12 . . . . 26}}$$

NOTE: Have chart in view, perhaps leaning against a flannelboard or on the wall.

ANNOUNCEMENT QUIZZES

A quiz provides an interesting method of making an announcement. A quiz can also be used to review announcement information, either immediately after an announcement has been given or after a time lapse.

I HAVE A QUESTION FOR YOU

Teacher quizzes puppet. Teacher, puppet, and children supply information.

First Week
#1: I have a question for you.
#2: O.K., what's the question?
#1: What's happening two weeks from Saturday?
#2: Well. . .I guess people will get up as usual. . .get dressed. . .do chores. . .call a friend maybe. . .
#1: No. . .NO. . .NO-O-O! Something special's happening. . .what is it?
#2: I don't know. (TO GROUP) Any of you kids know what's happening two weeks from Saturday?*. . .Nobody knows what's happening two weeks from Saturday. How about telling us?
#1: The all-church picnic is happening. . .that's what!
#2: WOW. . .great. . .can all these kids go?
#1: Sure. . .it's for everybody.
*If children know, adapt script accordingly.

Second Week
#1: I have a question for you.
#2: O.K., what's the question?
#1: What's happening a week from Saturday?
#2: I've got a big circle around that day on my calendar.
#1: Tell me what's happening.
#2: (TO GROUP) Hey kids, let's all tell him together. . .Ready. . .altogether. . .(PUPPET WHISPERS ANSWER TO GROUP IF NECESSARY) The all-church picnic!

Third Week
#2: I have a question for you.
#1: Good, I like questions.
#2: What's happening this Saturday?
#1: I don't know!
#2: Yes you do. . .you're just funnin' me.
#1: (TO GROUP) Let's all say it together. . .Ready. . .altogether . . .The all-church picnic!

NOTE: This type of skit can be adapted and performed all in one meeting, with a time lapse between the three parts.

WHAT'S HAPPENING SATURDAY?

Teacher quizzes puppet. Teacher supplies information.

TEACHER: What's happening Saturday?
PUPPET: (IN LOUD WHISPER TO TEACHER) I don't know. Tell me.
TEACHER: (IN LOUD WHISPER TO PUPPET) There's going to be a hike.
PUPPET: (CLEARS THROAT, THEN SPEAKS NORMALLY) A-hem. . . Would you please repeat the question?
TEACHER: What's happening Saturday?
PUPPET: There's going to be a hike.
TEACHER: What time is everybody supposed to meet at church?
PUPPET: (IN LOUD WHISPER TO TEACHER) I don't know. Tell me.
TEACHER: (IN LOUD WHISPER TO PUPPET) At 1:30.
PUPPET: (CLEARS THROAT, THEN SPEAKS NORMALLY) A-hem. . . Would you please repeat the question?
TEACHER: What time is everybody supposed to meet at church?
PUPPET: At 1:30. I sure know a lot about next Saturday, huh?
TEACHER: You do now!

WHAT'S HAPPENING WEDNESDAY NIGHT?

Teacher quizzes puppet. Children supply information.

TEACHER: How's your brain working today?
PUPPET: Just great, as usual. . .I think.
TEACHER: You think you're pretty smart?
PUPPET: Yep. . .maybe.
TEACHER: Let's find out how much you know about Wednesday night.
PUPPET: O.K.
TEACHER: Who's going to be right here in this room at 7 o'clock?
PUPPET: Uh. . .uh. . .(TO GROUP IN A LOUD WHISPER) Hey, kids, who's going to be here Wednesday night at 7 o'clock?. . .Are some of you going to be here?. . .Will some teachers be here?. . .Thanks. (TO TEACHER, AS IF HE KNEW ALL THE TIME) A bunch of kids and some teachers, that's who.
TEACHER: Why will they be here?
PUPPET: Uh. . .uh. . .(ASKS GROUP) A bunch of kids and some teachers will be here at 7 o'clock Wednesday night because that's the time for Kid's Club. Kid's Club is great fun you know, and kids learn something too.
TEACHER: Yes, I know.
PUPPET: And what they learn is all good stuff.
TEACHER: Yes, I know. Say, you sure did a good job of answering my questions.
PUPPET: I have to admit I had some help from my friends.
TEACHER: It's nice to have friends.
PUPPET: Kid's Club is a good palce to make friends. I hope there will be a whole big bunch of these kids here Wednesday night at 7 o'clock.
TEACHER: Me too.

CHILDREN QUIZ PUPPET

The three preceeding announcement quizzes are performed with the teacher doing the quizzing. However the same type of quiz can be conducted with children doing the quizzing.

Questions for children to ask a puppet can be provided in the following ways: (1) Teacher whispers the questions, one at a time, to individual children or to the group who then ask the puppet each question. (2) Print questions on chalkboard or large paper for individual children or the group to read. (3) Write questions on slips of paper for individual children to read. (4) Children think up their own questions.

The puppet can answer questions or ask for help from the teacher before answering. The puppet can answer correctly or incorrectly, perhaps giving a ridiculous answer. Even if puppet has asked for help, he can answer incorrectly and have to ask again. As a general rule, incorrect events or places voiced by the puppet should be less desirable than the actual event or place—so children will not be wishing they could go to the suggested event or place instead of to what is being announced.

TEACHER QUIZZES CHILDREN

When a teacher quizzes children concerning announcement information, a puppet participates by supplying unknown information to children as soon as the teacher asks them a question. If information is already known, puppet announces that the children answered correctly. Or puppet might disagree with a correct answer and have an outlandish idea as to what the answer might be. Teacher or children would set him straight.

PUPPET DOES THE QUIZZING

After an announcement has been given, a puppet can make sure it has been understood and remembered by quizzing individual children or a group, a teacher (even the one who gave the announcement), or another puppet. Information that is unknown, or pretended to be unknown, is supplied on request by puppet conducting the quiz or by whoever is not being quizzed.

Friend Puppet Says "Goodbye!"

At the closing of a session—besides sending children home with a warm feeling about Sunday School—a puppet can reinforce the emphasis of the day, give a reminder or stress a desired concept. Have one or more puppets address the group as a whole, or be stationed at the door and make remarks to individuals or small groups as they leave.

GOODBYE REMARKS
Limit remarks to one or two per session.

"Remember, God loves you."
"Will you try to remember to pray every day this next week?"
"Remember to read your take-home paper."
"All of us love you and hope you'll come back next Sunday."
"Tell the story of Moses to somebody today."
"Everybody try to bring your parents to the special meetings this week."

GOODBYE POEM

PUPPET: Our Sunday School is over (boo-hoo), but
I am glad to say
That we'll be here next Sunday;
Now have a nice day.

'Bye everybody.

I'LL NEVER SEE THESE KIDS AGAIN!

PUPPET: (CRIES, PAUSES, CRIES, PAUSES, CRIES) Boo-hoo-hoo.........boo-hoo-hoo........boo-hoo-hoo......
TEACHER: What's the matter?
PUPPET: I'll never see these kids again!
TEACHER: Why not?
PUPPET: Sunday School is over and they're all going home!
TEACHER: Yes, but they'll be back next Sunday.
PUPPET: Seems to me you've told me that before!
TEACHER: I tell you that quite often!
PUPPET: Then how come I keep forgetting?
TEACHER: I'll never know!
PUPPET: But maybe the kids will forget to come back next Sunday.
TEACHER: They're smart kids; I don't think they'll forget.
PUPPET: I feel lots better now. I sure do like these kids. 'Bye, kids. . .see you all next Sunday.

GOODBYE QUIZ

PUPPET: Let's find out how well you listened today.

SAMPLE QUESTIONS

1. Who can tell me the name of the second song we sang?
2. Who knows the third word of the memory verse?
3. Give me the names of two people in the Bible story.
4. What did Daniel learn about God in the story?

EVALUATION

Well, it seems you listened well (fairly well) today.

CONDUCTING A GOODBYE QUIZ

Questions can be asked of a group as a whole or of children singled out to be quizzed. Or a group can be divided in half—perhaps with the girls (or those with a last initial of "A" through "M") competing against the boys (or those with a last initial of "N" through "Z").

If one side is too far ahead, give easier questions to the other side (not obviously). Or try to arrange for the losing side to win the next week.

If a group is quizzed as a whole, and a question is not answered correctly, give one more opportunity. Then have the puppet either give the answer or ask that question again at the end of the quiz. If the answer is still unknown, the puppet could give hints before giving the answer.

If the puppeteer can't see the audience and children are to raise their hands, have an adult leader outside the stage call on children. The adult leader my have to repeat the answers so the puppeteer can hear them. A stage with a see-through viewing screen is helpful for a quiz.

4

Puppets in Neutral-Story Dramatizations

What is a neutral story? A neutral story is a true or fictitious story that does not involve a personal relationship with God on the part of any story character. Most neutral stories do not mention God at all. However, one character in a neutral story might tell another character a Bible story, and they might talk about God in relation to real people, but not in relation to themselves.

Neutral stories can be *believable* or *fanciful*. The plot of a true neutral story, such as an incident in the life of George Washington, is of course believable (true-to-life). The plot of a fictitious neutral story can be believable, such as a happening concerning two children at school; or the plot of a fictitious neutral story can be fanciful (not true-to-life).

Neutral Stories in Christian Education

A neutral story should be used to support the Bible story. It should not take the place of a Bible story. With the exception of lengthy allegories for special occasions, a neutral story should be kept short compared to the time allotted for the Bible story.

The neutral story should support the application desired. As we plan to present a neutral story, we as Christian puppeteers must ask ourselves, in honesty before the Lord, "If I were a child, what truth from God would I remember from this puppet presentation?" If the story does not sufficiently support the application, it would be wise to choose another story.

A number of types of neutral stories can be used in Christian Education. Among them are the following.

Point-of-contact stories. These are stories used as a point of contact for the purpose of gaining the children's attention before teaching a Bible story. You may often find this type of story at the beginning of a Sunday School lesson in a teacher's manual. Included in this type are conduct stories (stories that parallel the lives of children concerning the right way to think and live) and other stories that set the stage (establish common ground, introduce a concept, provide background information, pave the way) for solid Christian teaching. *This is the main use for neutral stories in Christian education.*

Fantasy stories. This is the type of story found in children's literature. Occasionally a short (2 or 3 minute) segment or summary of a carefully chosen fantasy story—such as Peter Rabbit—might be used during a Sunday School hour to illustrate a Bible truth. A longer fantasy story could be used during an extended session or in a Christian day-care situation. If a fantasy story is used, note the following guidelines:

1) Choose a story that clearly supports Christian truth.
2) Explain that the story is not true, if young children are in the audience.
3) Make sure children understand the application to Christian living. After the story is told, it is important to have a good discussion about the application in regard to people. Do not apply any spiritual truth to the story characters. In regard to the Peter Rabbit story you might say: "If you were in a situation like Peter Rabbit, what would God want you to do?"

Fables. Fables are fantasy stories written expressly to enforce some useful truth or guiding rule of behavior. Most fables involve animals that talk and act like humans. Several of Aesop's fables could be used to illustrate Christian truth.

Fairy tales. Fairy tales are stories concerning fairies, dwarfs, magicians, ogres, etc. *They have no place in Christian education.*

Parables. A parable is a short fictitious story written for the purpose of presenting a moral or spiritual truth, but the truth is not specifically stated. After the puppet presentation, make sure the children understand the intended meaning by means of questions and discussion.

Allegories. An allegory is the same as a parable in that it is a story with a veiled meaning, but an allegory is longer and more complicated than a parable. Allegories such as *Pilgrim's Progress* and *The Chronicles of Narnia* can be used in Christian education because they illustrate Christian truth throughout.

Neutral-Story Dramatizations

Any type of puppet may be used for neutral-story dramatizations. Children enjoy seeing animal and fantasy puppets even more than people puppets. A dog and a friendly monster can have a problem sharing a toy, or plan to do something nice for someone, often more effectively than people puppets can. People puppets may be used in combination with other types, if desired. If a story is true and/or respect is due the characters, do not have animal puppets represent people.

When a neutral story is true and/or respect is due the characters, it is best to present the dramatization in as believable a manner as possible, following the guidelines given for Christian-story dramatizations. Otherwise, neutral-story characters can have comic voices and can exaggerate emotions (be extra happy, extra sad, extra anxious, etc.), and animals can "speak" and demonstrate human traits.

Friend puppets as neutral-story puppets. You may wish to have a separate set of neutral-story puppets to use specifically for neutral-story dramatizations, but it is not necessary. Some stories can be adapted so friend puppets may use their own names and be themselves in dramatizations involving characters with similar personalities. Or, if changes in identity are required, note the following paragraph.

One puppet may play different parts in separate plays. A puppet may play the part of Joe in one play, Mr. Ray in another, and Pablo in still another. Children (except preschoolers) usually accept changes in identity quite readily. If you feel it is necessary, an explanation can be given before the dramatization. Have either the puppet, an adult leader, or a narrator puppet explain that the puppet is going to pretend to be (play the part of) a certain character in the play. For preschoolers, change the puppet's costume and wig, or add an accessory (hat, hair bow, glasses, scarf, tie). If you feel the older children would appreciate these changes in the looks of a puppet that is assuming a new identity, by all means make the changes. Be sure to call the puppet by the new name early in the play.

Interaction between neutral-story puppets and people. A story written in a book, or shown on a screen, is a completely closed unit. There can be no interaction between the story characters and the readers or viewers. A puppet dramatization is also a complete unit, but a neutral-story dramatization need not be closed. Puppets can momentarily "step out" of a neutral story and interact freely with people.

When one puppet speaks to an audience, any other puppets on stage should either (1) exit and return as the puppet steps back into character, or (2) remain on stage, motionless and facing away from the audience until the interacting puppet steps back into character. The same puppet, or different puppets, can interrupt a dramatization more than once, but limit the number of interruptions and keep them short so the thought pattern of the story will not be lost.

If the audience is large, you might want to limit the interaction to puppets making side comments to the audience, comments that do not require a response from the audience. Otherwise, the puppet interacting with an audience in regard to a story might request one or more of the following responses: (1) comment on his past action; (2) advice concerning where he should go, what he should do, or how he should feel; (3) quotation of a Bible verse; or (4) discussion of similar problems children have.

This type of interaction encourages: (1) value-judgments on the part of children, (2) recall of material learned, and (3) application of truths previously taught.

NOTE: Questions asked of a group should require a simple answer, or there will be a confusion of response. Questions asked of an individual can require a more complicated answer.

After the interaction, the puppet decides to act upon, or politely reject, any advice or direction that has been given. Then he steps back into character and the dramatization continues as if the audience weren't there. If neutral-story puppets step out of a story and ask children for advice based on the Bible, be sure to follow the guidelines previously given concerning *Friend Puppets and the Bible*.

CAUTION: If a group is over-stimulated by audience participation, or if an audience is large and unpredictable, it is best not to have story puppets speak to children.

5

Puppets in Christian-Story Dramatizations

A Christian story is one in which at least one character has a personal relationship with God. Christian stories concern either historical or present-day people and may be either true or fictitious. Because the Bible is the history of God's dealings with people, all Bible stories are considered to be Christian stories, even though all of the stories do not mention God in relation to the story characters.

Subject Matter for Christian Stories

Two types of stories make up the subject matter for Christian stories.

Bible stories. Bible stories adapted for a puppet presentation should be kept true to scripture. Any extra characters or plot should be minimal, added with great care and in keeping with the rest of the Bible. Watering down truth or the teaching of error is something no Christian puppeteer should allow.

Fictional Christian stories. Fictional stories with a Christian theme should also be true to scripture. For instance, a fictional story about heaven should not attribute human failings to angels or infer that heaven is anything but an absolutely perfect and happy place for all inhabitants. No matter how "cute" a story is or how intriguing, we must scratch everything that is in contradiction to what the Bible teaches. We are responsible to God for what we teach through puppetry.

How to Present a Believable Story

Christian-story dramatizations should be presented in as believable a manner as possible. A believable (true-to-life) presentation supports the concept that the story is not about the puppets themselves, but about the people they represent. However, young children may need to be reminded that the story is about the people the puppets are pretending to be. Although puppets are not real (can't see, speak, etc.) and are not capable of performing certain actions, and props and scenery are not made to scale, an audience will accept a dramatization as believable if the following suggestions are kept in mind.

1. *Puppets are the only actors.* No person outside the stage takes the part of a story character. Mixing puppets and people destroys believability. (Once in a while there can be an exception to this, as when Noah names the animals a person outside the stage could name the animal puppets as they appear on stage.)

2. *People puppets represent people, and animal puppets represent animals.* Do not use an animal puppet to represent a person in a Christian-story dramatization. An animal does not have an eternal soul for which Christ died. Do not have animals speak (except for the Bible story of Balaam, and perhaps for the parable of the lost sheep; occasionally you might have animals speaking to each other such as the stable animals or two sheep on the Bethlehem hillside, but not to a person).

71

3. *There can be no interaction between Christian-story puppets and the audience.* A Christian-story dramatization is a "closed unit." Christian-story puppets interact only with each other. They are not even aware that there is an audience out there.

If you wish to interrupt a Christian-story dramatization briefly for the purpose of interaction with a person standing alongside the stage or with the audience, first have all story puppets exit. Then have a non-story puppet, or a person, interact with the audience to: (a) review what has happened so far in the story, (b) guess what will happen next, (c) quote a Bible verse that applies to the situation, or (d) think about what one or more story characters should do, such as: "What do you think Tawoonga should do?. . . Do you think he should talk to the missionary even though his father will beat him if he finds out?. . . Let's see what Tawoonga decides to do and why." The audience cannot change the course of events in a Christian-story dramatization as would be possible in a neutral story. The purpose of such interaction is to involve a child more deeply in a story and thereby make way for a stronger impact on the child.

4. *Narration.* Supply any needed narration by means of: (a) a person outside the stage, (b) a narrator puppet (not a story character puppet), or (c) the voice of an unseen puppeteer inside the stage. If Christian-story puppets remain on stage during such narration, have them "freeze" (remain motionless), unless they pantomime action described by the narrator. There should be no back-and-forth interaction between a narrator and Christian-story puppets. Any narration should be brief unless accompanied with pantomime action.

5. *Play is performed with dignity.* Dignity supports believability. A slapstick method of presentation does not support believability.

6. *True-to-life names.* Christian-story characters should not have odd names or names of well-known puppet characters—unless the story is true and the actual names are odd or the same as well-known puppet characters.

7. *True-to-life voices.* Use regular voices for most Christian-story characters. If a comical voice is used, the subtle teaching is that the person is of low mentality, scatterbrained, or in some other way less than normal. We should not abuse great men of God by leading children to believe they are comical personalities.

8. *True-to-life script.* Neither a true nor a fictitious Christian story, when dramatized, should contain anything a real person would not or could not do. And no dialogue should indicate that the actors are puppets (like mentioning what they are made of or that they have no legs or teeth).

NOTE: Because of the nature of puppets, we cannot avoid certain basic inconsistencies in puppetry. Puppets are not real, yet we make them appear to move, see, hear, think and speak. Therefore, in Christian-story dramatizations, when it comes to having a puppet represent a person who has a relationship to God, we should make the presentation as believable as possible.

Puppets to Use For Christian-Story Dramatizations

As mentioned previously, for Christian stories, people puppets represent people, and animal puppets represent animals, as animals are not candidates for God's great salvation. Don't choose puppets that young children consider to be comical (to be laughed at on sight) if this might hinder the message of the dramatization. Such a problem might be solved by introducing the puppet and stating the role it is to play before a dramatization.

Friend people puppets can become Christian-story puppets the same as they can become neutral-story puppets. If you plan to use a friend puppet as a Christian-story puppet, see the suggestion given under "Story Puppets" in Chapter 1.

When it seems necessary to use a puppet to represent Jesus in a Christian story, see our discussion of this matter and what to do about it in the section, "Story Puppets" in Chapter 1.

Adapting Scripts to These Guidelines

If you have a script that does not conform to the guidelines given here about puppetry in Christian Education, you may be able to adapt it by making a few changes, such as the following.

Changing neutral stories. If the script has animal puppets talking about God in relation to themselves, see if it is possible to change the wording so the relationship is between people and God. For instance: Instead of having an animal puppet say, "I can't see God, but I know He hears me when I pray," have the puppet say, "People can't see God, but He hears them when they pray."

Changing Christian stories. If the content of a story is Christian but the script calls for animal or thing puppets with odd names, change the puppets to people puppets and give them people names.

Correcting stories on tape. If a tape has an objectional word or two, muffle the word by saying a cover-up word at this point, or by clearing your throat or making some other noise.

Other Puppet Activities

Story puppets may be used effectively in other activities related to Christian-story dramatizations. Some of these activities are given here. You may think of many others.

Exaggerated plot stories. The general guideline in Christian dramatizations, as previously stated, is that Christian stories (including dramatized conversations) are to be believable. However, there is an exception to this guideline. For children old enough to understand the message, an unbelievable plot and/or fanciful characters can sometimes be used to emphasize a point and increase the understanding of a truth. Note the following examples.

Example #1: (To dramatize the need for balance in the Christian life.) A puppet who is all eyes (nothing on his head except eyes) represents a Christian who reads his Bible at home but doesn't go to church or witness. A puppet who is all ears represents a Christian who listens in church but doesn't read his Bible or witness. A puppet who is all mouth represents a Christian who is quick to witness, but who isn't well informed and makes ridiculous statements about God and the Christian life. In the dramatization the puppets voice their thoughts out loud to themselves, speak to each other and speak to non-Christians.

Example #2: (To visualize the truth that doing good works does not cancel sin.) Puppet #1 has a bag labeled "SIN" tied to one arm. Puppet #2 enters and #1 asks #2 why he has the bag. Puppet #2 quotes Romans 3:23 and explains that sin will keep him out of heaven. Puppet #1 tries to shake the bag off. Then he blames others for causing him to sin and says that they should have the bag instead of him. When these measures fail, Puppet #1 decides that it must be doing good works that cancels sin, so he thinks good thoughts (out loud) and does good deeds (or exits briefly, reenters and tells about good deeds he has done)—but all to no avail. Puppet #2 enters and Puppet #1 notices he has no sin bag and asks why. Puppet #2 quotes Ephesians 2:8-9 and exits. Puppet #1 exits praying, "Dear God, I'm sorry for my sin. I believe Jesus died for me and I receive Your gift of salvation." Puppet #1 reenters without the sin bag and expresses his joy.

Example #3: (To emphasize the need for Bible reading.) Two puppets are gossiping, making very outlandish remarks. Person outside stage asks them what they're doing. Puppets finally admit they're gossiping. Person says he thought they were Christians. Puppets say they are. Person asks if they've seen certain Bible verses concerning gossip. Puppets say, "No," so person shows puppets verses as he reads them. Puppets say, "Oops," then scold each other for lack of information due to neglect of Bible reading.

Play-acting. Play-acting is an informal dramatization technique used effectively with young children. It is simply one puppet acting out the part of one story character for his own pleasure—after the story as been told. The friend puppet doing the play-acting need not correspond in looks, age or character to the Christian-story person he is play-acting.

Sample Script for a "Play-Acting" Puppet

Puppet: Acting out the part of Joseph is going to be great fun. I'll walk back and forth so you'll know I'm out looking for my brothers. (WALKS) Here comes a man. (PUPPET ASKS CHILD TO STAND BESIDE STAGE AND PLAY THE PART OF THE MAN, OR PUPPET TALKS TO PRETEND MAN.) Say, Mister, have you seen my brothers?. . . You say they went to Dothan?. . .Thank you very much. (WALKS A FEW STEPS) Oh, I see my brothers. (WALKS A FEW MORE STEPS. TALKS TO PRETEND BROTHERS) Hi, brothers. Ouch! (STRUGGLING) Why are you taking off my coat?. . . (STRUGGLING MORE) Are you going to throw me in that old dry pit? What for-r-r? (PUPPET DISAPPEARS BEHIND STAGE) You can tell I'm in a deep hole because you can't see me. What does the story say I do now? That's right (or "Now I remember"). (CALLING) Brothers. . .brothers. Do you suppose they can't hear me? Listen. . .do I hear camels? (PUPPET ENTERS) My brothers are pulling me out of the well. They are going to sell me to those traders. How am I going to act out going to Egypt. . .O.K., I'll go across the stage and disappear out of sight. . . .

(To involve children in this type of activity, have the play-acting puppet ask the group for ideas on how to act out certain parts of the story. This could be done before the play-acting begins or could be done two or three times during the performance, as indicated in the above script.)

Puppets as reporters. When a puppet is thought of as an eyewitness to an event, and gives a report, this is merely the telling of a happening; it is not the dramatization of an event. A report might be given of events in either a neutral story or a Christian story.

Any type of puppet can be used as a reporter—animal, person, tree, flower, star, etc.

A puppet reporter could speak to: (1) a group, (2) a person nearby, or (3) another puppet.

A report can be given as the event is happening or anytime after the event takes place. If a reporter is pretending to be at the scene as an event is happening, he could briefly and periodically look behind him (perhaps over a wall placed directly behind him) and give a report—in segments.

In whatever manner a report is conducted, it should be short. A long report will not hold the attention of an audience.

Puppets in interviews. An interview can be an effective means of providing information. An interview could be used before a dramatization—to set the scene and provide background information. Such interviews should be kept short. Long interviews easily lose the interest of children.

The interviewer (one who asks the questions) can be any type of puppet or can be a person alongside the stage.

The interviewee (one who answers the questions) also can be either a puppet or a person alongside the stage. If the interviewer is a person, the interviewee is a puppet. If the interviewer is a puppet, the interviewee can be either a person alongside the stage or another puppet. A puppet interviewee should look as much like the person he is representing as possible. The puppet might wear a nametag—a card on a string hung around his neck.

Who can be interviewed? Interviewees can be: (1) puppets representing story characters, including Bible characters; (2) animals that might have been at the scene of an event; (3) puppets representing Christian heroes (past or present); (4) puppets representing missionaries or children of missionaries; (5) actual missionaries or their children; (6) puppets or actual church staff members who tell the duties of their office; (7) puppets or actual choir members who tell why they sing in the choir and how the choir operates; (8) teachers of adults, so children can become acquainted with their parents' teachers; (9) class members or guests who are to make an announcement, give a musical presentation or share their testimony.

Puppets with a Time Machine. To add interest to interviews with historical characters, use a time machine. To make a time machine, glue knobs, dials, etc., on the front and sides of a cardboard box. Cut out the back and half of the bottom of the box so a puppet can go inside after he pretends to push the knobs and turn dials. Or a child might be asked to turn knobs and dials. Tape-record sound effects or make rattle-bang noises by shaking money in a tin can, etc.

To interview Joshua: Puppet #1 programs the time machine and pushes the button for Joshua's time period. (It'll be more fun for children if Puppet #1 asks a child to operate the machine for him.) Or, after setting dials to "ON" and "GO," Puppet #1 (or the entire audience) gives a verbal command, "Take us to the time of Joshua." Then mild time machine noises begin.

After Puppet #1 steps inside the machine, it makes loud noises. When the noises subside, Puppet #1 steps out. Joshua (Puppet #2) enters the stage and is interviewed by Puppet #1. Or an incidental character (Puppet #3) enters and, after being questioned by Puppet #1, tells where to find Joshua. Puppet #1 and Puppet #3 exit in different directons; but before they exit Puppet #3 might escort Puppet #1 across the stage and say that Joshua is close by. Or, if Puppet #3 offers to take Puppet #1 to Joshua, both puppets exit in the same direction. After a count of 5, Puppet #1 and Joshua enter the stage for the interview.

For a surprise interview, have a puppet push the SURPRISE button on the time maching. After the machine noises subside, the interviewer talks to the puppet that appears, trying to find out where he is, who is living at that time, and what is happening.

Sometimes the time-machine makes an error. Occasionally, after the desired time button is pushed, the machine takes the visiting puppet to the wrong time period. On other occasions, the machine brings a historical character to the puppet working the machine—as the puppet starts to enter the machine, the person he wants to interview steps out of the machine. When the historical character asks questions he is quite surprised at our modern age. An Old Testament person would not know of Jesus' birth and death, or what the word *Christian* means, etc.

Be sure to use different puppets as the interviewer. It will be of more interest to children to have different puppets take turns operating the time machine, rather than using the same puppet to operate the machine each time it is used.

Puppets with a Present-Day-Places Machine. To have a puppet visit present day missionaries, etc., use a Present-Day-Places Machine in the same manner as a Time Machine.

6

Puppets' Behavior

Guidelines given here for puppet behavior, involving manners, mischievous and bad behavior, as well as types of language to use and the inclusion of humor in puppet scripts, apply to both friend puppets and story puppets. Children are imitators and we must be careful what we project to them.

Mischievous Behavior

There is a place in Christian education for puppets that exhibit mischievous behavior or bad manners (laughing too loud, etc.). These puppets may need scolding and correction. Mischievous behavior should not be overdone, however, especially in the presence of young children, as they imitate without judgment.

Bad Behavior

Bad behavior is different from mischievous behavior and great care must be taken when there is occasion to allow puppets to display bad behavior.

Mild bad behavior. This is when puppets are disrespectful, impudent, or continually "snippy." Even mild bad behavior should not be exhibited unless it is done to make a point. When you feel it is necessary for a puppet to be objectionable in order to make a point, keep these guidelines in mind.

1) Underplay the incident (make it brief—just enough to convey the idea).

2) Choose language that does not show blatant disrespect for either children or adults.

3) Let the puppet know the behavior is objectionable and have the puppet respond favorably.

Harsh words. Avoid harsh words. Even when puppets are disagreeing with each other or objecting to another's behavior, they should not use expressions such as "shut up," "stupid," or "You're a liar." Such expressions are neither necessary nor desirable. "Be quiet" can be used instead of "shut up"; "stupid" can be simply left out of a conversation; and "You're not telling the truth" can replace "You're a liar." Insults do not add to the effectiveness of a message and puppets should not unnecessarily present a bad example for children.

There are some exceptions, however:

1) If the purpose of a presentation is to point out that insults and rough talk are not desirable, a puppet may need to say a few carefully chosen objectionable expressions. In this case, make sure there is correction.

2) A puppet might refer to something he himself has done as "dumb" or "stupid."

3) There are occasions when a puppet might, in a friendly way, call someone else a word like "dummy," but this should not be overdone.

4) In ventriloquist routines, it seems to be the tendency to have the vent partner delight in insulting the ventriloquist. A certain amount of mild "put-downs" is acceptable, but

each should be followed with an admonition. Carefully think through any remarks concerning the physical features of a person when using mild "put-downs," however. For example, even though the person with the "big nose" or "big ears" laughs along with the audience, the hurt is there and it may be difficult to minister to him. Remarks questioning the moral or spiritual integrity of a person can cast a shadow. The power of suggestion is strong. A negative remark, although obviously not true, can cloud a person's testimony in the minds of some.

Strong bad behavior. Very seldom would there be occasion to allow a puppet to show strong bad behavior, when puppets are acting violent or malicious. Remember that being violent or malicious is not limited to action; expressing the desire is being verbally violent or malicious. A puppet should never even say anything like: "I'm so mad at him I'd like to beat him up and push him off a high cliff," or, "Let's set fire to her doll house—that'll teach her," unless it is done to make a point. When such a point is really considered desirable, then proceed cautiously, and with the following guidelines in mind:

1) Underplay the incident (don't give it much time in the script).
2) Use respectful language.
3) Follow with a strong emphasis on the undesirable consequences.

Language

The puppeteer has a responsibility to keep the language used by puppets in good taste.

Grammar. Generally, puppets should be good examples of correct speech. On occasion, however, a word such as "ain't" might be appropriate if the expression fits the character and the intent of the script.

Slang. Use caution and wisdom in the amount and type of slang allowed in any puppet presentation. This is especially important if the slang is used in reference to God and Jesus Christ. Expressions such as "neat" and "something else" can be used in reference to what God has done, and perhaps in referring to God, Himself; but it would not be appropriate to use some popular expressions of the day such as "God (or Jesus) is a great guy," or referring to God as "The Man upstairs" or "The main Man."

Children need to understand that God is contemporary and friendly, but they also need to learn respect for His holiness and greatness. If Jesus were to walk into the room, we would fall at His feet in adoration; we would not say, "Hi, Buddy."

Near swear words. Puppets should not say such near swear words as: *gee, gosh, golly, darn, dang or heck.* According to Random House and other unabridged dictionaries, "gee" is a euphemism (substitute word) for Jesus, "gosh" and "golly" are euphemisms for God, and "darn" and "dang" are euphemisms for damn, and "heck" is a euphemism for hell. Many people are not aware of this, but puppets should be good examples and should not encourage the use of such words.

Modern-day language for Bible story scripts. There is no reason to use formal or outdated language in Bible story scripts. The original manuscripts of the New Testament were written in Koine Greek, not in classical Greek. Koine was the language spoken by the common people of the day. The King James version of the Bible was translated into language that was common in England about 400 years ago. The many modern-day translations of the Bible are an effort to make the Bible more easily understood. If there is a question in regard to doctrine in these translations, it is a good idea to check the text in several translations, including the very reliable King James version.

Paraphrases of the scriptures do not attempt an exact translation. A paraphrase is an effort to say the same thing in different words, using idioms of speech to bring out the intended meaning of a passage. Any questionable portions of a paraphrase should be checked with translations of the Bible. Paraphrases of the Bible are very helpful in preparing Bible story scripts, as they provide story-telling words to use.

Humor

Puppets and humor go well together. God gave us a sense of humor and we should use it.

Humor in a teaching situation with friend puppets. Humor can be worked into a teaching situation in many ways. But humor is not a requirement. Children will enjoy puppets even when no humor is included. Nevertheless, whenever possible, it is a good idea to add some humor to a presentation, as humor is an effective means of gaining and keeping attention. Often children will learn better when humor is included in the teaching process.

Humor in story dramatizations with story puppets. If a story lends itself to a bit of situational humor, consider including the humor. Even in a "message" dramatization, humor can be your best friend. Some truths are easier to present, and may have more impact when wrapped in humor. However, we must use wisdom in the amount of humor used with a story. It should not be used to the extent that it overshadows the message. The lasting impression of a serious story dramatization should be the message, not the fun.

Humor is sometimes used in what is called "contemporary" Bible stories. A contemporary Bible story is one that introduces present-day manners and customs with Bible times—such as having the disciples stop at McDonald's for a hamburger, or having the boy Samuel take his baseball cards when he goes to live with Eli. It is assumed that an audience will still accept the modern-day story as "believable," understanding that humor is added to increase interest for the modern-day generation. The wisdom of using this type of humor is questioned by those who feel the dignity due a Bible story will be diminished.

If this type of story is used, sprinkle—don't saturate—the story with a contemporary setting. It is best not to present a contemporary dramatization to children who are too young to understand the humor and who might think the story actually happened as told. For children, it would be a good idea to ask the audience to imagine with you how the story might have happened if it took place today, and make it clear that this is not an accurate account.

You might ask, "Must all puppet story dramatizations be sugar-coated and hilarious to be of interest to children?" The answer is no, quite the contrary. A puppet dramatization of a Bible story, of an incident in the life of a missionary, or even of two children learning to share, can be done very effectively without any humor whatsoever. A puppet story dramatization does not require humor any more than a story dramatized on a stage with people actors. Children respond well to serious drama. The reason for dramatizing a Bible story with puppets is not to prove that Bible stories are hilarious and Bible characters are funny. The reason is to aid in the teaching of the truths of the Bible.

What about the "punch line" at the end of a story dramatization? In some cases, a humorous punch line at the end of the script is advantageous. There is no need to conclude every puppet dramatization with a humorist twist, however. Sometimes, rather than diverting the audience's attention by having a sudden change at the end of the presentation, it is better to leave the audience pondering over the truth presented. This gives the Holy Spirit a bit more time to apply truth to minds and hearts.

General guidelines for using humor.

1) Humor should not dominate a learning situation—it should support, not take over.

2) Humor should not be used during the more serious part of a presentation, if it would lessen the impact of a message.

3) Humor should be geared to the age level of an audience.

4) Humor should have no ill-favor (in an effort to be funny, or for any other reason).

    a) Puppets should never make light of spiritual truths.

    b) They should not use ethnic jokes that could hurt feelings.

    c) They should not insult or belittle each other, except briefly, and then with a corrective admonition following.

    d) They should not speak disrespectfully of church leaders, parents, or any other person. This is for two reasons: (1) Puppets should not be a bad example to children. (2) Even though the person singled out may laugh at a remark, the hurt is there and it will make it difficult to minister to that person. Also, the insult or matter of disrespect can affect others in the same or similar circumstances.

5) The time for a series of appropriate jokes, or for a prolonged period of situational humor, is when puppets are being used mainly for entertainment.

7

Letting Puppets Teach

Children enjoy being taught by a puppet, especially when they are being taught Bible verses. Fun learning intensifies attention and provides a valuable aid in learning and retention of materials.

As you read the following ideas and skits you will discover that memorizing Bible verses is fun when they are taught by puppets. Some ideas and skits given here are designed only to introduce the words of a Bible verse, not to familiarize children with the words. These are simply starters. It is assumed that the puppet or the teacher will complete the teaching process in their own way. You will want to use many of the same methods in teaching other Bible verses.

Suggestions and Skits

SAY THE VERSE

Have you been searching for a new way to repeat a Bible verse to help the children learn it? Try this: display the verse on a sign and have a puppet enter, say the verse and exit. Have the same puppet, or another puppet, enter, say the verse and exit. Repeat this several times, varying rate of speech, volume, confidence or hesitancy in speech and position of the puppet in relation to the sign or the audience—face the audience not at all, sometimes, or all the time. Then have the puppet enter and say to the group, "How about saying this verse with me?" If clarification of  meaning is needed, have a puppet ask the children for help: "I'm not sure what those words mean. Can you tell me?" Or let the puppet do the explaining.

WRITE THE VERSE

Have a puppet hold a piece of chalk (felt marker), in his hands or mouth, and write the words on a chalkboard (piece of paper), as follows: (1) Puppet says the words as he writes them; (2) Teacher tells the puppet what to write; or (3) Children tell the puppet what to write.

CAN YOU GUESS THE WORDS?

PUPPET: I'm going to say a Bible verse, but I'm going to leave out some words. Let's find out how good you are at guessing. In II Corinthians 1:9, Paul is saying to the Corinthian Christians: "We should not ___(trust)___ in ___(ourselves)___ , but in ___(God)___ ." (IF THE FIRST WORD IS NOT GUESSED IN 3 OR 4

GUESSES, PUPPET GIVES HINTS* UNTIL IT IS. DO NOT PROLONG THE GUESSING. USE THE SAME PROCEDURE FOR THE OTHER WORDS)

*HINTS: The word starts with the letter "____." The word ends with the letter "____." The first syllable of the word is "____." The word sounds like "_____."

VERSE WHEEL

Attach the verse to a revolving sign. Have a puppet use his hand, mouth or head to revolve the sign as the verse is read. Or the puppet might ask a child to revolve the sign.

CAN YOU READ UPSIDE DOWN?

Ask a child to hold a partial circle over the sign so only the upside down writing shows and have all the children read it aloud. A puppet can revolve the wheel until the children have read the complete verse.

CAN YOU READ IN A CIRCLE?

Write the verse in a circle and have the children read it as a puppet revolves the sign.

SURPRISE!

(Adult leader goes out of room and returns at prearranged signal.)

PUPPET: Say, boys and girls, I see Mrs. Smith isn't here right now. Would you like to surprise her and learn the Bible verse for today? Then when she comes to teach it to you, you'll already know it. Wow! Will she ever be pleased! I read the verse in the Sunday School book this morning and worked real hard to memorize it, so I'm all ready to teach it to you. Bible verses are fun to learn. This one says . . .

(Or, if verse is posted in view of puppet and group, they could read and learn it together.)

FISHING HOLE

Needed:

Folded sign: FISHING HOLE

Black watercolor felt pen

Flannelboard or chalkboard

Fishing pole: Tie and tape string to end of stick. Form paper clip into a hook; tie and tape to string (or tie magnet to string).

Bible verse cards:
   Philippians 2:14: "Do all things without mur-murings . . ."

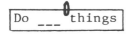

Make and letter cards as above, using heavy paper or cardboard. (Cardboard can be covered with white or colored paper.) Glue strips of flannel or paper toweling to back of cards so they will adhere to a flannelboard (omit if using chalk tray). Push a paper clip partway onto each card (see drawings) and tape in place.

PUPPET: Guess what someone gets to do today! (RAISE "FISHING HOLE" SIGN AND PLACE OVER STAGE). Go fishing! Sally, it's your turn. While you're coming up, I'll get the fishing pole. (PUPPET EXITS. RETURNS WITH POLE IN HANDS OR MOUTH. HOLDS POLE IN REACH OF CHILD) Now Sally, you go fishing and see what you get. (SALLY LOWERS HOOK INTO THEATER. PUPPETEER, OR HELPER, ATTACHES CARD TO HOOK OR MAGNET. PUPPET DIRECTS SALLY TO RAISE POLE, COMMENTS ON CONTENT OF CARD, AND DIRECTS ITS PLACEMENT ON FLANNELBOARD OR CHALK TRAY)

When all cards are in place, puppet, or teacher, leads children in guessing what letters or numbers are needed to fill in the blanks on the cards. Either a child or an adult fills in the blanks with felt pen or crayon. If missing letters or words are not guessed after a few tries, have someone start reading at Philippians 2:10 and stop after the word "murmurings" in verse 14. To speed up the guessing of a reference, tell children that the number of the verse is a little more than 12, or have chldren read Philippians 2 until someone finds the verse.

NOTE: If ink from pen might bleed through cards onto flannelboard, remove cards from flannelboard while filling in blanks.

IN, ON, UNDER, OR AROUND

PUPPET: It's memory verse time, and we're going to play a game. The name of the game is, "In, On, Under, or Around." The Bible verse is written on pieces of paper hidden around the room. I'll say a word that sounds like something in this room. You have to guess what that "something" is. One of the pieces of paper will be in, on, under, or around that "something."

PUPPET OR TEACHER (CONDUCTS GUESSING OF "CHAIR"): O.K., everybody* look in, on, under, or around your chair. . .Ah, Jane found a piece of paper taped under her chair. Jane, give the paper to Mr. Jones, and he'll give you a larger sign that has the same words on it. . . . Now, would you please come up front and hold your part of the verse high so we all can read the words?. . .The next clue word is "more." (Door) John, you guessed "door" so go look, in, on, under, or around the door for a piece of paper. . .(LET JOHN ENJOY THE INCONGRUITY AND FUN OF SETTING THE PUPPET STRAIGHT ABOUT LOOKING "IN" A DOOR.) . . . .Ahah! You found the paper taped behind the door, but it's too high for you to reach. You may either stand on a chair or ask Mr. Jones to reach it for you. . . . Now, exchange your paper for a sign, and come up front so we all can read the words. (PUPPET CONTINUES THIS ROUTINE UNTIL ALL PARTS OF THE VERSE ARE FOUND AND READ, AND THE VERSE IS READ AS A WHOLE. IF THE VERSE PARTS ARE OUT OF ORDER THE PUPPET COMMENTS ON THE STRANGE SOUNDING VERSE AND ASKS THE CHILDREN TO CHANGE POSITIONS. HE THEN TEACHES THE VERSE OR ASKS MR. JONES TO TEACH THE VERSE)

*If everybody looking is likely to cause confusion, have only one person look under all the chairs, or perhaps under just one chair such as the desk chair or the piano chair.

Additional clue ideas. "Cable," clue taped to side of table; "fox," clue in box; "gasket," clue taped to side of waste basket; "blue," clue in shoe inconspicuously placed on table in back of room.

HERE COMES A NOTE

TEACHER: It's memory verse time, and I don't know quite how to get started. (PUPPET ENTERS WITH NOTE IN HANDS OR MOUTH) Ah, here comes a note. Maybe this will give me a clue. (TEACHER TAKES NOTE AND READS IT ALOUD)

IDEAS FOR KINDS OF NOTES

Bible verse reference, and location of a hidden visual aid packet or verse design. The location could be behind a door or flannelboard, or under the piano, etc. A sign could be *complete* or *incomplete.* An incomplete sign would have blank spaces for the missing words. A puppet would: (l) comment, "Oops! looks like I forgot to write down all of the verse." Or he might (2) read the verse, or ask the group to read it, and say, "That doesn't sound right," or (3) ask the group to find the verse in the Bible and fill in the blanks. Or (4) excuse himself, exit and return with another note containing the missing words, not in order. The teacher might: (l) read the words and the group would decide where they belonged. Or (2) say, "I can't read this writing!" and then show the note to the puppet and ask him to read it.

Incomplete reference and one word of verse. This type of note might contain the book and chapter, but not the verse, and (1) the first word (see note in drawing). The puppet would comment, "That's all I had time for," or "all I could remember," and ask, "Who can find a verse that starts with 'But' in the first chapter of John?" (2) Or a word other than the first might be given. If a verse is not near the beginning of a long chapter, narrow the hunt to a few verses, e.g., somewhere between verses 30 and 37. After the verse is read, the puppet or the teacher could suddenly remember the location of a sign or visual aid packet, which the teacher or puppet could then use to teach the verse.

POPPYCORN

PROPS:

Attach three pieces of popcorn to stage using loops of tape with sticky side out.

(PUPPETS #1 and #2 ENTER. #1 LOOKS AT POPCORN)

#1: Yum, yum, I see some poppycorn. How about I eat it?

#2: You may have it, but you have to do something first.

#1: What? Tell me what I have to do.

#2: You have to say today's Bible verse.

#1: Tell me words . . . I say them.

#2: "Love one another . . . "*

#1: I can't say them.

#2: Try.

#1: I can't.

#2 and #1: (#1 REPEATING EACH WORD AFTER #2) Say: "Love (Love).......one (some) ....one (one) ....another (another)."

#2: Now say the whole verse.

#1: (SLOWLY) "Love one another." That right?....."Love one another." I get poppycorn now?

#2: O.K.

#1: "Love (EATS ONE PIECE**)...one (EATS SECOND PIECE)...another." (EATS LAST PIECE, EXITS FOR COUNT OF THREE, REENTERS AND TEACHES VERSE TO CHILDREN***)

(Voice offstage or person outside stage can take the part of #2.)

   * I Peter 1:22
 ** Puppet can "eat" by taking popcorn in mouth, chomping, and lowering head inside stage while dropping popcorn out of mouth.
*** If group is small each child could be rewarded with popcorn.

IF I JUST KNEW THE FIRST WORD

#1: It's time for me to teach you the Bible verse, but there's just one teensy little problem. . .I can't remember it. I studied it every day last week, and I knew it backwards and forwards. If I heard the first word I know it'd come back to me.

#2: (ENTERS) Hi-dee-hi-hi and how do you do?

#1: Did you say "do?" That's it—that's the first word. . ."do." (#1 THANKS #2

ENTHUSIASTICALLY, PERHAPS GIVING A KISS OR HUG)

#2: (TO AUDIENCE) What's so special about "do?" Maybe I ought to say "do" more often.

#1: O.K. I'm ready; I remember the verse now.

(#1 TEACHES PHILIPPIANS 2:14, OR IF VERSE IS PRINTED ON A SIGN, CONTINUE SCRIPT)

#1: Excuse me a minute; I think I'm going to sneeze. (EXITS)

#2: (PLACES SIGN ON STAGE) Hey, look what I found. Doesn't that first word say "Do?" (SNEEZE HEARD OFF STAGE)

#1: (ENTERS) Excuse the sneeze, please. (LOOKS AT SIGN) That's today's Bible verse. Where did you find that sign?

#2: In a box.

#1: You're sure handy to have around.

#2: I think you're right. . .'bye. (#1 TEACHES VERSE)

WPALSEMTWHN

#1: I'm going to say a Bible verse, and then let's see if you can say it. "Wherefore putting away lying, speak every man truth with his neighbor." Ephesians 4:25a Now you say it.

#2: Uh. . .uh. . .uh. . .

#1: Maybe this will help. (HOLDS UP SIGN OR PLACES SIGN OVER STAGE)

#2: (READING SIGN) W-palsem-twhn?* I don't think that's the verse you said.

#1: Sure it is.

#2: W-palsem-twhn?

#1: No, those letters are the first letters of the words in the verse. Each letter will help you to remember the word that comes next. In Ephesians 4:25a, the Bible says to all people, "Wherefore putting away lying, speak every man truth with his neighbor."

#2: Don't people tell the truth all the time?

#1: I'm afraid not, but God wants people to tell the truth all the time. Can you say the verse?

#2: "Wherefore putting away. . ." (TO GROUP) I forgot the word that starts with "L". (GROUP OR PUPPET #1 SAYS "LYING") "Wherefore putting away lying, speak every man. . ." (HESITATES, LOOKS AT GROUP, GROUP OR PUPPET #1 SAYS "TRUTH") "Wherefore putting away lying, speak every man truth with his. . ." (GROUP OR PUPPET SAYS "NEIGHBOR") "Wherefore putting away lying, speak every man truth with his neighbor. Ephesians 4:. . ." (GROUP OR PUPPET #1 SAYS "25a") (PUPPET SAYS VERSE) How about you kids saying the verse with me this time? (PUPPET AND GROUP SAY VERSE)

Puppet #1 or #2 could ask a child to explain the meaning of the verse in his own words and might ask individuals to say the verse.

*To pronounce, say the letter "W" and add an "e" to "twhn" (twhen). If the first letters of words in other verses cannot be grouped into pronounceable syllables, vowel sounds can be added between letters, and a limited amount of letters can be said by themselves, as the "W" at the beginning of this verse.

EAT OR READ

PROPS: Three cardboard pancakes with words (see script) or scribbles on them. Box: Cut slit in shoebox just wide enough to fit over stage. Cut hole in back of box for passing of pancakes. Or, if stage has flat ledge for box to sit on, cut shoebox to measure 2" high. Then no hole in back of box and no assistant is needed.

TEACHER: (OUTSIDE STAGE) I have some puppet pancakes. I think I'll put them right here, and whoever comes along can have them. (PLACES CARDBOARD PANCAKES IN BOX. ASSISTANT IN STAGE TAKES PANCAKES THROUGH HOLE IN BACK OF BOX.)

#1: (ENTERS, LOOKS IN BOX) Oh, boy! Pancakes. . .big, beautiful pancakes. I gonna eat 'em all up. M-m-m-m-m. . .Hey, what kind of pancakes are these? They have words on them!

#2: (ENTERS, LOOKS IN BOX) Words, oh, boy! Let me read them.

#1: No, I gonna eat 'em.

#2: No, I'm going to read them! (THEY ARGUE)

#2: I have an idea; I'll read them and then you eat them.

#1: Good idea. Hurry up. . .I hungry!

#2: (LOOKS IN BOX TO READ WORDS ON FIRST PANCAKE) "Be content. . ." (ASSISTANT IN STAGE HOLDS PANCAKE THROUGH HOLE IN BACK OF BOX. #2 TAKES AND GIVES TO #1)

#1: (EATS PANCAKE*) Yum, yum, yum, yum, YUM-M-M!

#2: (READS SECOND PANCAKE) ". . .with such things. . ." (GIVES PANCAKE TO #1)

#1: (EATS PANCAKE) Yum, YUM.

#2: (READS THIRD PANCAKE) ". . .as you have" Hebrews 13:5. (GIVES TO #1)

#1: (EATS PANCAKE) YUM. (SAYS VERSE THREE OR FOUR TIMES)

#3: (ENTERS) What are all those words I'm hearing?

#2: Those words were on the pancakes he ate, and he seems to be filled with the words. . . can't seem to say anything else!

#3: You'd better find some more of those pancakes; those are wonderful words he's saying. Those words are from the Bible.

NOTE: (The part of Puppet #3 can be taken by a person outside the stage.)
*To eat pancake: puppet chomps, momentarily dips head below stage (or turns back to audience) and drops pancake, then continues chomping with nose held high.

ANSWER "YES" OR "NO"

Have a puppet ask questions before a verse is taught.

PUPPET: Do you think Jesus said to His disciples, "Worry I leave with you"?. . .Or do you think He said, "Peace I leave with you"?. . .Or do you think He said, "Joy I leave with you"? Find John 14:27 in your Bible (or listen to the teacher read John 14:27), then tell me what He said.

BALLOONS

PROPS: Four balloons, each tied to a stick or straightened coat hanger. Number four small pieces of paper and tape to ends of sticks or coat hangers. Write reference and portions of verse (see script) on four 1"x5" strips of paper, index cards or lightweight cereal box cardboard. Roll up strips and insert one in each balloon; lay out balloons so verse is in order. Blow up balloons and tie to sticks or coat hangers at opposite end from number (see script for order of sticks).

Balloon popper: a push pin (pin with plastic holder or thumbtack taped to a popsicle stick.

Four signs (see script for words). If stage is narrow, you may make signs as in illustration at right or print words on strips of paper, back with flannel or paper toweling and use on flannelboard. Have puppet direct placement of signs on flannelboard. Or ask children to hold signs.

PUPPET: I'm in the mood for a balloon.* Anyone see a balloon around here anywhere? (PUPPET DOES NOT LOOK AT BALLOON THAT APPEARS BESIDE HIM. GROUP TELLS PUPPET ABOUT BALLOON) Where?... (LOOKS AT BALLOON, SPEAKS EXCITEDLY) Oh, sure enough, there's a balloon! I wonder if there's a "rattely"** inside. A rattely is a piece of paper, with words on it, that rattles inside a balloon. (BALLOON JIGGLES SO NOISE IS HEARD) I heard a rattely, I did...yippee! Did you hear the rattely? I just have to get the rattely out. Where's my popper? I remember, Mrs. Swanson has my popper.*** Johnny, would you ask Mrs. Swanson for the popper and pop the balloon for me? Oh, I can hardly wait. (CHILD POPS BALLOON. RATTELY FALLS TO FLOOR) Where'd the rattely jump to? Find it, Johnny, and read it (or give to a teacher to read, or hold so I can read). What does it say?.. "happy is he." Just a minute, I'll be right back. (EXITS, RETURNS WITH SIGN) Look what I found. What does this say? (GROUP READS "HAPPY IS HE") That's what I thought this sign said. (PLACES SIGN ON STAGE) Do you suppose this is part of a Bible verse? I sure hope so, but how can we find the rest of the verse.. .or whatever this is? (2ND BALLOON APPEARS) Ahah!, another balloon! (REPEAT PROCEDURE UNTIL ALL SIGNS ARE IN PLACE)

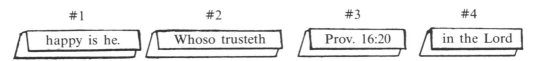

#1	#2	#3	#4
happy is he.	Whoso trusteth	Prov. 16:20	in the Lord

Now let's read this. (GROUP READS) H-m-m-m, that doesn't sound quite right to me. (PUPPET REARRANGES CARDS, PERHAPS INCORRECTLY, THEN CORRECTLY, OR ASKS CHILD TO REARRANGE THEM. GROUP READS VERSE SEVERAL TIMES UNDER PUPPET'S DIRECTION)

*Or puppet sniffs and says, "I smell a balloon. . .I know I do. I smell a balloon."
**Pronounced "ra'-tuh-ly."
***For variety, if script idea is used on different occasions, popper could be on top of the piano, taped under a chair, etc.

NOTE: You might want to have the balloon dodge being popped once or twice before holding still. If your group is over-stimulated by audience participation, have the puppet (not a child) pop the balloon.

SCRIPTURE SCRAMBLE

Displaying signs out of order, as in the balloon skit, is a type of Scripture Scramble. The balloon introduction is not necessary, however. Just place signs over a stage, out of order. Have one or more puppets rearrange the signs several times incorrectly, asking the children each time, "Is this right?" One puppet might drop a sign out of the theater and ask a child for help to replace it.

A variation to the Scripture Scramble idea is to have only parts of words on signs and the signs out of order. Do not use periods or capital letters that would indicate the position of the sign, except for capital letters on the names of deity.

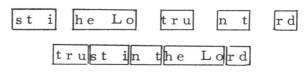

Another type of Scripture Scramble is to have a puppet say a short verse with the words out of order, e.g., "Love God is" for "God is love." The teacher could write the words on a chalkboard or large paper as the puppet says them, or the puppet could hand out flannel cards in mixed order.

Write a number on the back of each sign indicateing the correct order so the puppeteer will know when the signs are lined up correctly.

I LEARNED IT, CAN YOU?

The verse has been taught to the puppet by the teacher while the children listened.

PUPPET: Were you listening while I learned the verse? I know it really, really good now. I might even be able to say it backwards. Let me try. (TURNS BACK TO GROUP AND QUOTES VERSE) Didn't think I could do it, did you? Anyway, now it's time to teach you the verse frontwards. Do you think you can learn it as well as I did? (PUPPET TEACHES VERSE, PRAISING CHILDREN FOR THEIR EFFORTS) Now would you like to hear me say the verse backwards. . .for real this time? (ATTEMPTS TO QUOTE VERSE BACKWARDS BUT FAILS) Why am I doing this? Nobody can understand a verse when it's said backwards. Bible verses are full of so many wonderful words that it doesn't make sense at all to say one backwards. Let's all say the verse again. . .frontwards. Ready for the first word. . . .

SURPRISE BOX

PROPS: Cloth-covered box is set over stage or held by puppeteer. Bible verse is printed on front of box.

#1:   (ENTERS, LOOKS AT BOX) What's this? (#2 ENTERS. #1 LOOKS AT #2, AT BOX AND BACK TO #2) What's that?

#2:   (LOOKS AROUND) What's what?

#1:   (LOOKS AT BOX) What's this?

#2:   A surprise box. . .Pull off the cloth.

#1:   (PULLS CLOTH A BIT, JUMPS BACK) Will something jump out and bite me?

#2:   No. (#1 PULLS OFF CLOTH)

#3:   (POPS UP) Surprise. I bet you didn't expect to see me! (LOOKS OVER FRONT OF BOX) This is the Bible verse for today. I get to read it, and then Mr. Collins is going to teach it. I'm very good at reading upside down. The verse says. . . . (#3 READS VERSE)

NOTE: To make box that sets over a stage, see directions in the "EAT OR READ" skit.

SHY SIGN TIME

("P and G" refers to PUPPET AND GROUP)

PUPPET: Is everybody ready? Ready for what, you ask? Ready for the shy sign, that's what. Everybody say, "It's shy sign time." Altogether now. . .

P and G: It's shy sign time. (BIBLE VERSE SIGN QUICKLY ENTERS AND EXITS)

PUPPET: That sign sure is shy; it only faced us for a second or two. Can anyone tell a word that was on the sign? (GROUP RESPONDS) Let's try again. Everybody say, "It's shy sign time." Altogether now. . .

P and G: It's shy sign time. (SIGN REPEATS ACTION)
PUPPET: How many words can you say now? (GROUP RESPONDS)

(REPEAT ROUTINE UNTIL SIGN IS READ, HOLDING SIGN IN VIEW LONGER EACH TIME IF NEEDED. IF VERSE IS LONG, REPEAT ROUTINE UNTIL FIRST LINE OR TWO ARE READ. SIGN SHOULD EXIT ABOUT FOUR TIMES)

PUPPET: Strange thing about this sign, after the sign is read (or first line or first two lines are read) it usually isn't shy any more. Let's call the sign again and ask if it will stay with us. Altogether now. . .
P and G: It's shy sign time. (SIGN ENTERS)
PUPPET: (TO SIGN) Are you going to stay with us this time? (SIGN DIPS AS IF TO SAY "YES") Good. (TO GROUP) Now we can learn the verse.

(PUPPET OR TEACHER HAS GROUP READ VERSE AT DIFFERENT SPEEDS, THEN WITH BOYS AND GIRLS SAYING WORDS ALTERNATELY. AFTER SEVERAL READINGS, SIGN EXITS)

PUPPET: Oops! I guess the sign has decided it's time to find out if we can say the verse by ourselves. You all try real hard to say it right. (GROUP, WITH OR WITHOUT PUPPET, SAYS VERSE. IF VERSE IS REPEATED CORRECTLY, SIGN REMAINS OUT OF SIGHT.) We must have passed the test because the sign didn't come back. Good for us. We deserve a handclap; everybody clap. (GROUP CLAPS) Well done. (IF VERSE IS REPEATED INCORRECTLY, SIGN RETURNS AND PROCEDURE IS REPEATED)

THAT'S NOT MUCH OF A VERSE!

#1:   (ENTERS, PLACES 1ST SIGN OVER STAGE* AND READS) "For God. . ."
#2:   (ENTERS) What are you reading?
#1:   A Bible verse.
#2:   (READING) "For God. . ." that's not much of a verse!
#1:   There's more. (ADDS 2ND SIGN AND READS) ". . .so loved. . ."

#2:   "For God so loved. . ." What did God love? I wonder what God loved.
#1:   (ADDS 3RD SIGN AND READS) ". . .the world. . ."
#2:   "For God so loved the world. . ." Is that the whole verse?
#1:   (ADDS 4TH SIGN AND READS) ". . .that he gave. . ."
#2:   "For God so loved the world that he gave. . ." What did God give?
#1:   Not what—who—who did God give? (ADDS 5TH SIGN AND READS) ". . .his only begotten Son. . ." Do you think that's the end?
#2:   Nope, I think there's more. This verse keeps getting better and better.
#1:   (ADDS 6TH SIGN AND READS) ". . .that whosoever believeth in him. . ."
#2:   "For God so loved the world that he gave his only begotten Son, that whosoever believeth in him. . ." Hurry! I can hardly wait for the next words.

90

#1: (ADDS 7TH SIGN AND READS) "...should not perish but have everlasting life."
     John 3:16.
#2: I just knew those words would be great. (QUOTES VERSE) Just think, every boy
     and girl and older person who believes in Jesus has everlasting life! That's exciting!
     That's fantastic!

*Or signs can be placed over stage all together and removed one at a time. (See
drawing.)

WHERE COULD THAT VERSE BE?

PUPPET: (DISTRESSED) I've been asked to teach the memory verse today, and I can't
         find the paper it's written on. Betty, would you look in the piano bench?...It's
         not there? Now where could that verse be? Teachers and kids, would you be
         kind enough to look through all your things?...No one found it? Well, I just
         don't know where it could be. (PUPPET TURNS BACK TO AUDIENCE;
         PAPER IS TAPED TO BACK OF PUPPET. GROUP DISCOVERS PAPER
         AND TELLS HIM) Thanks kids, you saved the day for me. Roger, would you
         please take the paper off my back and hold it so I can read it? Only I can read
         it, you know; it's written in puppet language!

WANT SOMETHING SPECIAL?

#1: Want to hear something special?
#2: Yeah!
#1: (SLOWLY) Psalm 18:30, "As for God, His way is perfect." 'Ya got that?
#2: Yeah.
#1: Well then, give it back.
#2: (SLOWLY, WITH #1 SUPPLYING FORGOTTEN WORDS) Psalm 18:30, "As
     for...(God),...his...(way)...is...(perfect)."
#1: Say it again.
#2: Psalm 18:30, "As for God, his way is perfect."

#1: 'Ya got that now?
#2: Yeah.
#1: Don't you ever forget it!
#2: (EXITS SAYING VERSE, PAUSES, ENTERS AND ASKS IF A CHILD CAN SAY THOSE SPECIAL WORDS)

ALPHABET SOUP

PROPS: Bowl: Cottage cheese carton cut to fit over stage.
      Small measuring cup
      Plastic spoon
      (Tie cup and spoon to puppets' arms.)*

BOY: (ENTERS, LOOKS AT BOWL) Yum. . .alphabet soup. . .don't need this letter. (SLURPS SOUP, FIDDLES AROUND WITH SOUP, SLURPS SOUP. MOM ENTERS) Mom, could I have a little more soup, please?

MOM: No sooner said than done. (EXITS, ENTERS, POURS SOUP FROM MEASURING CUP INTO BOWL) That should warm it up for you.

BOY: I didn't want to warm it up. I just wanted enough letters to spell out the Bible verse for this week.

MOM: Oh, so that's it. . .what is the Bible verse?

BOY: Isaiah 2:4b "Nation shall not lift up sword against nation, neither shall they learn war anymore."

MOM: Do you have enough letters now?

BOY: Not quite.

MOM: (EXITS, ENTERS, POURS SOUP) Did you get the letters you need?

BOY: Yep. (SLURPS SOUP) And I ate all the ones I don't need. See if I did it right.

MOM: (LOOKS IN BOWL AND READS VERSE**) Yes, all the letters are there.

BOY: That's a really good verse, Mom, but I wonder when it's going to come true.

MOM: I don't know. Let's ask the teacher.

BOY: After she tells us, maybe she'll let me help teach the verse to the boys and girls.

*If puppets are not capable of arm movement, have Mom pretend to pour soup by standing near bowl and have Boy blow soup instead of "fiddle around." Have Boy drink soup from bowl, making an excuse for not using a spoon: "Excuse me for not using a spoon, but we're all out of spoons in our house today."

**Instead of gathering the verse letters in the soup bowl, the puppet could take letters out, turn his back to the audience and busy himself momentarily. Then a sign could appear with real alphabet soup letters against contrasting paper, spelling out the verse.

Rewards for Learning

PRAISE

Children should be praised for work well done. They will be especially delighted if the reward of praise comes from a puppet.

PUPPET: It's Bible verse time. I'm not going to stay while you learn the verse, but I'll be back soon and listen to you say the verse. You'll have to say it over and over to learn it really good—so you won't make any mistakes—tah-tee-tum-tum, 'bye. (WHEN PUPPET RETURNS HE GIVES PRAISE ACCORDING TO EFFORT MADE BY GROUP)

PRIVILEGE

WORK A PUPPET. As a reward for knowing a verse, let the child use a puppet to say the verse to the class. Most children will count this a distinct privilege, and it is an aid to further learning.

FEED A PUPPET. For each verse said, let a child give a puppet a treat such as a cardboard cookie or an unshelled peanut. The puppet need not swallow the treat. He could chomp with great delight and duck his head out of sight, dropping the treat behind the stage. Or he could drop it in a box, or ask the child to drop it in a box, and say, "This looks so good, I'm going to save it for later." A box could be attached to a theater or on a chair outside the theater.

GIVE OR RECEIVE AFFECTION. For each verse said, allow the child to give a puppet a hug, a kiss, a "pat" on his nose or the top of his head, or a scratch behind his ear. Or a puppet might give any of these to the child.

MEMENTO

Children will be pleased if a puppet rewards them with a memento for saying a verse. This could be a trinket, a peanut, a Bible bookmark or just a strip of colored paper, perhaps with a gold star attached.

Application of a Verse

The following skits show how puppets can be used to illustrate and apply the meaning of the verse.

WATCH MY CANDY

#1:   Will you watch this candy for me? I will be right back.
#2:   Sure. (#1 EXITS) Look at that nice candy. I'm going to watch it go right into my mouth. (EATS ONE PIECE) Boy, was that good!. . . He'll never miss one. . .I

wonder where he is. (LOOKS AROUND) Maybe just one more piece of candy. (EATS) Still not back. . .I'll take just one more piece. (EATS) I guess he's going to be late. . .I'll take another piece. (EATS) Oh, no, they are all gone! Now what will I do?

#1:   (ENTERS) Hey, where is my candy?

#2:   I don't see any candy.

#1:   I thought I told you to watch it for me.

#2:   I did.

#1:   Then where is it?

#2:   Look in here. (OPENS MOUTH) Do you see anything?

#1:   No.

#2:   That's funny, they were there just a minute ago.

#1:   You mean you ate them!

#2:   I guess so. But I watched them the whole time, going into my mouth, then I lost sight of them.

#1:   I'll never trust you again. NEVER. (#1 AND #2 EXIT)

#3 and #4:   (ENTER)

#3:   He was a bad boy; he stole candy.

#4:   (NODS HEAD) The Bible says, "Thou shalt not steal." Numbers 20:15

NOTE: Since this script is showing a wrong doing, there should be care not to give it an atmosphere of comedy—especially when presenting it to young children.

EASY AND NOT SO EASY

#1:   (TO #2) "This is the day which the Lord hath made; we will rejoice and be glad in it." Psalm 118:24.

#2:   (TO GROUP) We're supposed to make up two skits about this Bible verse, and we're waiting to hear what the first one is about.

VOICE OFFSTAGE: Sunny day. . .pancakes and bacon for breakfast.

#1:   O.K., this will be easy. (#1 AND #2 TURN AWAY FROM GROUP, WHISPER BRIEFLY TO EACH OTHER, THEN FACE GROUP AND YAWN)

#2:   Good morning. Guess I'll look out the window and see what kind of a day it is. (WALKS TO SIDE, LOOKS OUT) Ah, a beautiful, sunny day, how nice. "This is the day which the Lord hath made; we will rejoice and be glad in it." Psalm 118:24.

#1:   I wonder what's for breakfast.

#2:   Let's go find out. (THEY EXIT, PAUSE, ENTER)

#1:   Our favorite breakfast—pancakes, yum-yum!

#2:   And bacon. (TAKES DEEP BREATH) Just smell that bacon cooking! Ah-h-h-h.

#1:   "This is the day which the Lord hath made; we will rejoice and be glad in it." Psalm 118:24.

#2:   I have a feeling our next skit isn't going to be so easy.

VOICE OFFSTAGE: Rainy day and oatmeal.

#1:   You're right. This is going to take a little thought. (THEY TURN AWAY FROM GROUP, WHISPER A LITTLE LONGER THAN BEFORE, FACE GROUP, TURN AWAY AND WHISPER BRIEFLY, THEN FACE GROUP AND YAWN)

#2:   Do you hear something?

#1:   Yeah, sounds like rain. . .and when it rains we can't play outdoors.

#2:	But the garden needs the rain, and maybe we can put that model together today.
#1:	Good thought. "This is the day which the Lord hath made; we will rejoice and be glad in it."
#2:	I wonder what's for breakfast.
#1:	Let's go find out. (THEY EXIT, PAUSE, ENTER)
#2:	(DISGUSTEDLY) Oatmeal! Our most un-favorite!
#1:	Uh-huh. Remember, bacon is expensive; we can't have it every day. And oatmeal is good for us.
#2:	Good thought (ENTHUSIASTICALLY) "This is the day which the Lord hath made; we will rejoice and be glad in it." Psalm 118:24.
#1:	(TO GROUP) Let's all say that verse together. (#1 AND GROUP SAY VERSE)

LET ME TALK TO MYSELF ABOUT THIS

JACK:	Oh, here comes that pesky little Tommy. (TOMMY HOPS ON JACK'S BACK) Don't do that! I don't want to give you a piggy-back ride. . .Get down and go away.
TOMMY:	Oh, please. . .just a short ride. Just a short ride, Jack, please.
JACK:	Let me talk to myself about this, O.K?
TOMMY:	O.K.
JACK:	(TALKING TO HIMSELF) Jack, remember that "Even a child is known by his doings. . ." Do you want to be known as unfriendly, grouchy, and having no time for little kids?. . .No, I don't want to be known as unfriendly, grouchy, and having no time for little kids. Older kids like me should take some time to play with little guys like Tommy. (TO TOMMY) Tommy, forget what I said about getting down. I'll take you for a jolly, bumpy, piggy-back ride. Here we go. (AS THEY EXIT) "Even a child is known by his doings. . ." Proverbs 20:11.

Challenge To Be Creative

Take the ideas given in this chapter and let them stir your imagination to create more ideas and write scripts of your own. You might begin by taking ideas from two or more scripts and combining them into one script. For instance, combine elements of FISHING HOLE and HERE COMES A NOTE. Use the fishing hole but bring up one or more cards that have a part missing. The puppet could say, "It looks like a fish took a bite out of this card. I guess you'll have to look this verse up in your Bibles."

As you experiment and write, remember:
1) Puppet presentations usually should be short and to the point.
2) Humor should serve its purpose, but should not dominate a teaching situation.
3) Puppetry is merely a tool to bring divine truth to life in children's lives.

8

Children Teach Puppets

Children enjoy assuming the role of a teacher and teaching Bible verses to a puppet. And such teaching involves learning on the part of the child. The ideas and sample skits that follow give several variations to the basic idea of teaching a puppet.

Suggestions and Skits

WHISPER A VERSE

After being taught a verse, young children, each in turn, can whisper the verse to the teacher's puppet. Have the puppet repeat the verse either correctly or making a mistake such as: "Jesus went down the road doing good" instead of "Jesus went about doing good." Children enjoy having a puppet make mistakes, and this, of course, leads to more repetition of the verse as the children correct the puppet.

CAN YOUR PUPPET SAY THE VERSE?

In one four-year-old department, each child is given a puppet. As the teacher says the words of the memory verse, each child teaches the verse to his puppet. Then the teacher calls on the puppets to recite the verse. This results in more participation and retention of the verse than before puppets were used.

MOMMY, CAN I HAVE A PEANUTTY?

A puppet does not need an incentive to learn a Bible verse other than just the joy of knowing a verse, but occasionally you may wish to make use of an incentive such as food. The following script can be used with any two puppets, or any puppet and a person outside the theater.

CHILD: Mommy, can I have a peanutty?
MOTHER: You may have a peanut if you can say today's Bible verse to me without making any mistakes. (EXITS)
CHILD: I sure wish I knew the Bible verse, 'cause yum-yum, I'd sure like to have a peanutty. Do you kids know the verse? . . .Would you teach it to me, huh, would you? (GROUP TEACHES VERSE: PUPPET MAKES A FEW MISTAKES BEFORE SAYING IT CORRECTLY) Did I say it right, huh, did I? . . .Oh, thanky, thanky, thanky for teaching me the verse. Now I'll get a peanutty.
MOTHER: (ENTERS) Can you say the verse? (CHILD SAYS VERSE INCOR-RECTLY) Sorry, that's not quite right. (EXITS)
CHILD: Would you say that verse to me just once more, please? (GROUP SAYS VERSE. MOTHER ENTERS) I know the verse. . .I really know it now. (SAYS VERSE)

MOTHER: Very good. . .that's exactly right.
CHILD: Can I have my peanutty now?
MOTHER: You surely may. There's a peanut in the cupboard.
CHILD: (EXITS SAYING) Yum-yum, I just love peanutties. Thanks kids for teaching me that verse. Yum-yum, I just love peanutties.
        (Peanut could be taped to stage and eaten by puppet in view of group.)

TEACH ME THAT VERSE

A junior church superintendent discovered that his children learned a Bible verse unusually well and in a fun way when he had them teach the verse to an enthusiastic, but slow-learning puppet. By the time the puppet could say the words correctly, so could all the children.

Print the verse on a chalkboard, large sheet of paper, or smaller paper taped together. Teach the verse briefly and leave it in view of children. If children are too young to read, the teacher should tell them the words so they can teach the puppet.

If you do not wish a group to participate in the teaching of a slow-learning puppet, have a second puppet teach him. Children will learn by hearing the learning process. If limited group participation is desired, have the teaching puppet occasionally ask for help from the group or from individuals within the group.

If children are too young to read, the teacher should supply the words when needed.

SWASH: That was a great Bible verse you just learned. . .Deuteronomy 12:25. Do you suppose you could teach it to me? I hope so 'cause I sure do like to learn Bible verses, but sometimes I have trouble. You tell me the words when I ask; and say, "That's wrong, Swash," if I make a mistake, and, "That's right, Swash," if I get the words right. . .O.K.? Here we go. Tell me the first five words.
GROUP: "Do that which is right. . ."
SWASH: Do everything right. . .Did I say it right?
GROUP: That's wrong, Swash.
SWASH: Wrong? What was I supposed to say?
GROUP: "Do that which is right. . ."
SWASH: I'll get it right this time. . ."Do that which is right. . ." Is that right?
GROUP: That's right, Swash.
SWASH: Good. Now I'm ready for the next three words.
GROUP: ". . .in the sight. . ."
SWASH: Do that right in sight. . .How'd I do?
GROUP: That's wrong, Swash.
SWASH: Really? I thought sure I had it. O.K., tell me again.
GROUP: "Do that which is right in the sight. . ."
SWASH: "Do that which is right in the sight. . ."
GROUP: That's right, Swash.
SWASH: So far, so good. Now for the last three words.
GROUP: ". . .of the Lord."
SWASH: ". . .of the Lord."
GROUP: That's right, Swash.
SWASH: Yeah, I just knew it was. Now for the reference. Where's the verse found?
GROUP: Deuteronomy 12:25.
SWASH: Deuteronomy 12:25. . .Right?
GROUP: That's right, Swash.
SWASH: (TAKES A DEEP BREATH) Now for the whole verse. Uh. . .you'd better say it first.

GROUP: "Do that which is right in the sight of the Lord." Deuteronomy 12:25
SWASH: Do that which is right in God's sight. Deuteronomy 12:25
GROUP: That's wrong, Swash.
SWASH: How could that be? I tried hard. Well, this time I'll try harder. Are you ready? Here I go. (CLEARS THROAT) "Do that which is right in the sight of the Lord." Deuteronomy 12:25
GROUP: That's right, Swash. (GROUP MIGHT CLAP AND PERHAPS RING A BELL)
SWASH: (TWISTING AND JUMPING AROUND) Wow! I knew I could do it if I tried hard enough. You did an excellent job of teaching. Thanks a bunch. I'm not the easiest guy in the world to teach, you know! (SERIOUSLY) My, but those are good Bible words for you kids to know. I hope you all try to do what is right in the sight of your Lord. . .all day. . .every day.

Types of mistakes for this type of script are: omit a word, add one or more words, reverse the position of two words, substitute an incorrect word for the correct one. Choose any mistakes carefully. If your children interpret this type of teaching as making fun of God's Word, or if they are likely to make these types of mistakes on their own when being taught by other means, then limit the puppet's learning problem to simply forgetting words, perhaps forgetting the same word several times even after saying it correctly. The puppet could ask for help, or just hesitate and wait for children to supply the next word.

When using this type of skit with other verses, make sure the puppet does not make the type of mistakes that would result in ridicule of the Bible verse. Also, don't allow the mistakes to be frequent enough to confuse the learning of the verse.

On occasion, the puppet might surprise himself by learning a verse without making any mistakes. This would add variety and would be a help if time is short or if the memory verse is especially long or difficult.

If you wish, the puppet can bring out the meaning of a verse as he learns it by asking questions or making short comments.

The script need not be continued, but the following addition will further reinforce the learning of a verse.

            You know what? My friend, Swish, likes to learn Bible verses as much as I do.
SWASH: Too bad I can't ever find him. (MOVES TOWARD END OF STAGE) If I could find him, I'd teach him this verse.
SWISH: (ENTERS) Hi, kids. (QUICKLY EXITS. NEITHER PUPPET SEES THE OTHER)
SWASH: (LOOKING AROUND) I thought I heard Swish's voice, but I don't see him anywhere. Well, if you see Swish, will you teach him the verse? I'll go look for him. (EXITS)
SWISH: (ENTERS) My, what a nice looking group of boys and girls. (IF THE GROUP TELLS SWISH ABOUT VERSE, SKIP THE NEXT THREE SENTENCES) You look like you'd like to teach me something. I hope it's a Bible verse. Am I right?. . .Tell me the first five words. (SWISH SAYS THE VERSE, PHRASE BY PHRASE, WITH NO MISTAKES) Now let's see if I can say the whole verse. Maybe you'd better say it with me first.

GROUP AND SWISH: "Do that which is right in the sight of the Lord." Deuteronomy 12:25

SWISH: "Do that which is right in the sight of the Lord." Deuteronomy 12:25. Oh joy, oh delight, I know another Bible verse. You certainly are good Bible verse teachers. Thanks a lot. 'Bye now. (EXITS)

SWASH: (ENTERS) Did you see Swish?. . .Did you teach him Deuteronomy 12:25? Are you sure you taught it to him right? Say it one more time for me, O.K.?

GROUP: "Do that which is right in the sight of the Lord." Deuteronomy 12:25

SWASH: You kids are marvelous, just marvelous. Thanks for everything. 'Bye.

TWO-FACED PUPPET

Instead of two separate puppets, a two-faced puppet can be used for the continuation of "Teach Me That Verse." To make a two-faced puppet, add facial features to the back of a puppet's head. Eyes can be black felt circles glued to larger white felt circles; a nose can be a chenille pom-pom (ball fringe); a mouth can be of felt, but may not be needed. A hairbow will denote a girl. If a puppet has long hair, attach the features to, or through the hair; the second face will be a monster-type puppet.

If a puppet has long fake-fur hair over the entire head, you might name the puppet "Harry" (because he's hairy), and the face on the back of the head could be his sister, "Harriet."

To operate a two-faced puppet, turn the back of your hand toward the audience. If the puppet has mouth action, opening the mouth will cause the face on the back of the head to nod. An audience will interpret this as "talking." When one puppet turns his back to an audience to go look for the other, the other automatically faces the audience.

If a group tells a puppet that the other puppet is in back of him, have him look behind him and say, "Nope, there's nobody there." If they say the second puppet is on the back of his head, he exclaims, "That's impossible. Whoever heard of having someone on the back of your head!" If they say, "Look in a mirror," have the puppet say, "If I saw someone on the back of my head in a mirror, I wouldn't believe it. That's just impossible."

HAVE YOU SEEN MY FRIEND?

The following three skits are similar. The basic idea involved has been so effective in the teaching of Bible verses that all three skits are included for the purpose of variety.

SKIT 1

RINGER: (ENTERS CALLING) Parsley. . .P-a-r-s-l-e-y. (LOOKS AT GROUP) Oh, hi. My name's Ringer and I have a problem. I can't find my friend, Parsley. Have you seen her? (DESCRIBES PARSLEY IF NEW TO GROUP). . .No? I'll go look for her. (EXITS)

PARSLEY: (ENTERS CALLING) Ringer . . .oh, Ringer. . .Ringer. (LOOKS AT GROUP) Hi. Say, have you seen Ringer?. . .You have?. . .I want to ask him if he'll teach me a Bible verse. Which way did he go?. . .Thanks. (EXITS IN DIRECTION GIVEN)

RINGER: (ENTERS CALLING) Parsley. (LOOKS AT GROUP) Hello again. Did Parsley come by here?. . .She did?,. . .Where is she now?. . .I'll tell you why I want to find her. She likes to learn Bible verses and I just memorized this really great verse. I'd like to teach it to her. How about if I teach you the verse and then, if Parsley comes back here, you teach the verse to her, O.K.? (RINGER TEACHES VERSE TO GROUP) Remember now, if Parsley comes here, you teach the verse to her. I'll keep looking. (EXITS, PAUSES, ENTERS) Did you see her yet?. . .Maybe I'd better check to make sure you still know the verse. Say it for me one more time. (GROUP SAYS VERSE.

PUPPET GIVES ADDITIONAL TEACHING IF NEEDED. SPEAKING ENTHUSIASTICALLY) Very good. VERY GOOD. V-E-R-Y G-O-O-D! You're all ready for Parsley in case you see her before I do. (EXITS)

PARSLEY: I thought I heard Ringer's voice. Was he here? (IF GROUP IS HESITANT, PARSLEY ASKS IF RINGER ASKED THEM TO DO ANYTHING. PARSLEY MAKES MISTAKES LEARNING THE VERSE. RINGER RETURNS BEFORE SHE CAN CORRECTLY QUOTE THE VERSE.)

RINGER: (ENTERS) Hi, Parsley. Are the kids teaching you the Bible verse?

PARSLEY: They're trying but I'm having a little trouble.

RINGER: Try saying the verse to me.

PARSLEY: (QUOTES VERSE INCORRECTLY. VOICE OFF STAGE CALLS FOR RINGER.)

RINGER: I hear someone calling me. I'll be back as soon as I can. (EXITS)

PARSLEY: Quick, help me learn the verse right. (CHILDREN TEACH VERSE. PARSLEY QUOTES IT CORRECTLY) Ooooh, I can't wait 'til Ringer comes back. Maybe if I call him, he'll hurry. (PARSLEY WALKS TO ONE SIDE OF STAGE CALLING FOR RINGER. RINGER ENTERS WITH HIS BACK TO PARSLEY'S BACK. BOTH WALK BACKWARDS TOWARD EACH OTHER AND BUMP AT CENTER STAGE. BOTH SHOW SURPRISE AND ASK THE OTHER'S PARDON. PUPPETEER WILL NEED TO CROSS HANDS TO ACCOMPLISH THIS. OTHER-WISE HAVE PUPPETS LOOK AT AUDIENCE AND NOT LOOK AT EACH OTHER. MOVE THEM TOWARD EACH OTHER SIDEWAYS UNTIL THEY BUMP.)

RINGER: Do you know the verse yet?

PARSLEY: I think so.

RINGER: Let me hear you say it.

PARSLEY: (QUOTES VERSE CORRECTLY)

RINGER: You did it! Did you say, "Thank you" to the boys and girls?

PARSLEY: Thanks much. Wouldn't it be great if all of you taught that verse to somebody else today?

SKIT 2 (SHORT VERSION)

#1: I know a Bible verse. But you probably wouldn't know this one. (PUPPET OR TEACHER PROMPTS GROUP TO ASK WHAT VERSE AND TELL PUPPET THEY KNOW IT—CLASS JUST LEARNED VERSE) Do you kids know everything? I was sure you wouldn't know that verse. I've been trying to find (name of another puppet) so I could teach him that verse, and I can't find him anywhere. If you see him, will you teach him that verse for me? I'd sure appreciate it. 'Bye. (EXITS)

#2: (ENTERS) Hi, everybody. (GROUP TEACHES VERSE TO #2. #1 RETURNS AND IS SURPRISED THAT #2 ALREADY KNOWS THE VERSE.)

SKIT 3

BOOKER: Hi, I'm Booker and I'm looking for Clue. Have you seen her? . . .I'll go look some more. (EXITS)

CLUE: (ENTERS) Hi, I'm Clue. I have a feeling somebody's looking for me. Is anyone looking for me? . . .He is? . . .O.K., I'll go look for him. (EXITS)

BOOKER: (ENTERS) Has Clue been here? . . .I want to find her because I'd like to teach her that Bible verse you just learned. Clue loves to memorize Bible verses. If you see her tell her to *wait right here*, O.K.? (EXITS)

CLUE: (ENTERS) Hi again. (CLUE OR ADULT LEADER PROMPTS GROUP IF NECESSARY) Say, how about if you kids teach me that verse* while I'm waiting. Tell me the first three words. (CHILDREN TEACH CLUE PHRASE BY PHRASE. SHE MAKES A FEW MISTAKES BEFORE QUOTING VERSE CORRECTLY)

BOOKER: (ENTERS) I finally found you. The boys and girls must have told you to wait for me.

CLUE: Yep.

**BOOKER: Want to learn Ephesians 6:1?

CLUE: Nope.

BOOKER: (SURPRISED) NO?. . .Why not?

CLUE: I already know Ephesians 6:1. (GIGGLES) Want to hear me say it? (QUOTES VERSE WITHOUT WAITING FOR BOOKER TO ANSWER)

BOOKER: Did these kids teach you the verse?

CLUE: Yep. Want to hear me say it again? Better yet, want to hear us all say it together?

BOOKER: Sure do.

CLUE: O.K., kids, all together now. . .(CLUE AND GROUP QUOTE VERSE)

BOOKER: Thanks, kids, for teaching Clue. What a great verse for you to know.

CLUE: I hope all of you say this verse to yourselves 168 times this week. . .and also think about what it means.

BOOKER: Let's see. . .7 goes into 168. . .twenty-four times. So they'd be saying the verse 24 times every day!

CLUE: What's wrong with saying a verse 24 times a day?

BOOKER: Not a thing. . .not a thing. . .In fact, that's a very good idea. Anyway, what I plan to do next week is to ask some of you if thinking about this verse during the week changed your thinking or your actions in some way.

*Have the verse on a flannelboard or printed on a sign or chalkboard in view of the group. Or have an adult leader prompt the group if necessary.
**Alternative ending for script:

BOOKER: I know how you love to learn Bible verses and I'm ready to teach you another great verse. Repeat after me, "Be content. . ." (First 2 or 3 words of your current verse)

CLUE: "Be content with such things as you have" Hebrews 13:5. (Your current verse)

BOOKER: Am I hearing things? I thought I only said, "Be content."

CLUE: You did. "Be content" is all you said.

BOOKER: Then how come you said, "Be content with such things as you have" Hebrews 13:5?. . .(SUSPICIOUSLY) Did these kids teach you the verse?

CLUE: Yep. How about that?

BOOKER: You did a good job, kids, thanks.

INVOLVE CHILDREN IN THE APPLICATION

When you involve children in acting out or discussing the application of a Bible verse, the truth of the verse is more deeply impressed on their minds. Two good methods for involving children for this purpose are given here.

1. *Have a puppet state a life-situation problem and ask for help.* For example: "My brother lost a dime, and I found it. I want to keep that dime, but I'm not sure I should. Do you know a Bible verse that would help me decide what to do?" Or, you could have two or more puppets act out the problem.

TYPE OF VERSE TO USE. When a puppet is involved in making the application, use moral conduct verses, such as: "Do all things without murmurings (Philippians 2:14)." "Even a child is known by his doings (Proverbs 20:11);" "Be content with such things as ye have (Hebrews 13:5);" and "Be willing and obedient (Isaiah 1:19)."

TYPE OF VERSE NOT TO USE. Since a puppet is not a human being capable of a personal relationship with God, a puppet does not have an eternal soul. Therefore, do not use verses that have to do with salvation, God's care of people, trust in God, serving God, or expressions of thanks to God when using a puppet to help make the application.

If you wish to use a verse such as "Serve the Lord with gladness (Psalm 100:2)," have a puppet tell of a person he knows who has a problem. For example, "I know a boy named Randy. When it was Randy's turn to clean up after paper-cutting time in Sunday School, he did it, but he stuck out his lip and was mad the whole time. Do you know a Bible verse that would help Randy?"

BIBLE VERSE PUPPET. A Bible verse puppet is very useful. This is a puppet who can only say, or shake his head, "Yes" and "No" and say Bible verses. Have children call, or ring a bell, for his appearance. An added feature can be a large cardboard Bible that he reads from. When a problem is posed, children can call for the BIBLE VERSE PUPPET to give the Bible verse to the puppet(s) who needs help.

2. *The children can use puppets to act out a possible solution to a problem stated by the teacher.* Before the puppet presentation, conduct a class discussion on how the verse you wish emphasized might be applied, or give the student puppeteers time for discussion away from the main group, or both.

TYPE OF VERSE TO USE. Any type of verse can be used for this purpose if the following guidelines are followed:
1) Make it clear to the children that the puppets are only representing real people.
2) Give the puppets names to fit the dramatization.
3) Don't include interaction between puppets and audience.

COACH CHILDREN'S PUPPET PRESENTATIONS. If children become embarrassed because they don't know what to say or do when they are acting as puppeteers, the purpose of the presentation by children (to impress a truth on their minds) might be lost. Therefore, any time a student puppeteer hesitates too long during a puppet presentation, the teacher should provide ideas or tell the child the exact words to say and actions to perform. A puppet manipulated by the teacher could do the coaching. Children do not seem to mind being prompted, but they do mind being embarrassed.

APPLICATION OF A VERSE TO THE LIFE OF A CHILD. After children have applied a Bible verse to a problem under discussion, ask them to think of ways to apply the same verse to their own lives.

Memory Verse Reviews

Children are more likely to retain memory verses if they review and review and review them. Puppets can help in this review time. When a puppet is helping to review a verse, it should show enthusiasm and be delighted when children quote verses correctly.

1. *Review of a verse taught the same day.*
LATER, DURING A SESSION. Have a puppet say, "I wonder if I still know today's memory verse." Let the puppet make one or two mistakes and ask the children to teach him again. Or ask the group to say the verse with him. A puppet might do this two or three times during the hour.

AT THE END OF A SESSION. Have a puppet stationed at the door asking children as they leave to tell him the Bible verse they learned. Puppet should refresh their memory, if necessary, and encourage endeavor at home.

THE FOLLOWING WEEK. As the children enter the room, a puppet could ask each child if he can say the "secret passwords" (last week's memory verse). An honor sticker could be awarded.

A review center might be set up in another area where a teacher would re-teach the verse to those who do not remember it, so all children could have the fun of saying the "secret passwords" to the puppet. An honor sticker of a different type could be awarded to those who need a second chance.

If the puppet used for reviewing a verse is the same one who had trouble learning it, he might comment, "I may have trouble learning a verse, but it's a funny thing that at the end of Sunday School and all the time after that, I know it really well."

2. *Review of several verses.* If you review several verses each week, a puppet could use one or more of the following methods.
   1) Say verse and ask for reference.
   2) Say reference and ask for verse.
   3) Say first word, or any word, in verse and ask for complete verse.
   4) Hold up sign showing first word, or any word, in verse and ask for verse.
   5) Hold up sign showing first *letter* of each of first few words of verse, holding sign in view very briefly, then longer each time, until verse is recognized.
   6) Have puppet state a life-situation problem which is answered by one of the verses and ask for the verse that would help.

3. *Skit to eoncourage review of a Bible verse during the week.*

PUPPET: Hi.
TEACHER: Hi. Do you know the Bible verse we learned last week?
PUPPET: Well. . .I'm afraid not.
TEACHER: Why not?
PUPPET: I didn't say it every day, the way you said to do.
TEACHER: Why not?
PUPPET: I couldn't find the paper it was written on for awhile.
TEACHER: What do you mean, "for awhile"?
PUPPET: The paper was lost Monday and Tuesday, but I found it on Wednesday. When I found it I said, "Hi, paper," and put it in a special place, the way you said to do.
TEACHER: Then why don't you know it?
PUPPET: I've been busy.
TEACHER: Busy doing what?
PUPPET: Well. . .just busy.
TEACHER: Were you too busy to watch television?
PUPPET: Well. . .no.
TEACHER: Then were you really too busy to review your verse?
PUPPET: Hm-m-m, when you put it that way, no, I wasn't too busy, was I? You sure know how to make me think about things. I'll review the verse this week, and I'll know it next week. . .I really will. You just wait and see.

Follow through, and have the puppet know the verse the following week. After a few weeks, you might repeat this script, using a different excuse, perhaps one the children have given you.

9

Puppets Help Children Sing

Children of all ages enjoy singing for a puppet. The suggestions and scripts given in this chapter are for all children, but you may need to adapt a script aimed specially at younger or older children to the age needs of your particular group.

Puppets to Use in Singing

Friend puppets should sing only "puppet songs." *Puppets songs* are songs that declare truth but do not involve a personal relationship with God on the part of the singer. Songs such as: "God Can Do Everything," "Everybody Ought to Love Jesus," and "Jesus Loves the Little Children of the World" are puppet songs.

Story puppets may sing either "puppet songs" or "people songs." *People songs* allow for a personal relationship with God by the character whose part a puppet is playing. These include such songs as: "Oh, How I Love My Lord," "Wounded for Me," "A Child of the King" and "Jesus Loves Me."

Use only people puppets to represent people; do not use monster-type puppets to represent characters in a skit or to sing "people songs." Remember, when a story puppet sings, it should have no interaction with the audience.

Puppets Listen to Children Sing

A puppet listening to children sing provides for puppet participation in songs inappropriate for a friend puppet to sing. However, do not limit listening to "people songs." Children enjoy doing their best when a puppet is listening to their singing.

You may wish to indicate that a puppet is listening and enjoying the singing by having him keep time to the music. A puppet could move his head in a "U" pattern, tilt his head from side to side, tap a hand or clap his hands in rhythm. Movement should be minimal for a quiet song, and in no case should the puppet detract from the intent of the song.

Reasons for Listening

Puppets need no special reason for having children sing to them, but on occasion you may wish to invent one, such as the following.

SORE THROAT   (Puppet has scarf wrapped around his throat.)
PUPPET: (WHISPERING) I've been looking forward

to singing with you today but, as you can see, I have a sore throat. I've tried, but I just can't sing. (OPENS MOUTH AND MAKES ROUGH NOISE) So, would you sing some songs for me? I'd sure enjoy hearing you sing.

UPSET STOMACH

PUPPET: (MAKES EXAGGERATED NOISES AS IF IN PAIN)

TEACHER: What in the world is wrong with you today?

PUPPET: I think maybe my breakfast doesn't like me.

TEACHER: What did you eat for breakfast?

PUPPET: I'd rather not talk about it.

TEACHER: Why did you come to Sunday School if you're in such pain?

PUPPET: Well. . .I thought if I heard some good Sunday School singing, I'd feel better. (AFTER GROUP SINGS ONE SONG) I think I feel a little bit better. How about another song? (AFTER SECOND SONG) I'm sure I feel somewhat better now, but could you please sing one more song? (AFTER THIRD SONG) Say, I'm feeling terrific. How about that! Thanks a bunch, kids.

HEADACHE

PUPPET: I have a headache today. I could take an aspirin, but what I think would help most would be to hear some especially good Sunday School singing. Do you know where I could go to hear some?

TEACHER: You don't have to go anywhere! You can hear some really good singing right here. (CHILDREN SING)

PUPPET: Thank you. . .my headache is much better, but I think it needs one more song. (AFTER SECOND SONG) Ah, my head feels just fine. You boys and girls are very good singers.

NOTE: Another puppet can take the place of the teacher in the above two skits.

TO EVALUATE SINGING

Most children will give extra effort to singing well if they know a puppet is listening. One primary choir director found a puppet to be very effective as an aid to discipline and incentive for quality singing. The puppet didn't like noise; when it was quiet he appeared and announced that he was going to listen to the singing from within his puppet house (anywhere out of sight). He was interested in how well he could understand the words, and in the pleasing tones. The choir was more orderly and sang better than before, yet the director had used only a mouse finger-puppet.

In a Sunday School situation you would probably not have a puppet evaluate singing as for a choir, but children do like to hear a puppet express pleasure in listening to them sing. If the singing is poor, a puppet could express disappointment and ask for the song to be repeated. A puppet might evaluate by holding up a sad face, an O.K. face, or a happy face. Or he could ask his "evaluator machine" to pop up a face.

A DESIRE TO HEAR A CERTAIN SONG

A puppet can ask the teacher to please have the children sing a certain song or the puppet can ask the group directly.

PUPPET: I sure wish I could hear somebody sing (name of song). All week I've been wishing I could hear some kids sing (name of song). Does anyone here know that song? Would you sing it for me?

GIVE AND TAKE

PUPPET: I like to sing. Oh, yes I do. I like to sing to you and you. Also I like to hear you sing to me. Let's do this: First you sing a song to me, then I'll sing a song to you, then we'll sing a song together. . .this is going to be fun.

Puppets Visualize a Song

Visualize a song by showing something that illustrates the song during the singing. This may be objects attached to a stick, or words, pictures or drawings pinned to a signboard. If a signboard is covered with flannel, items backed with pieces of flannel or paper toweling will adhere to the signboard.

PUPPET: Watch the stage as you sing this next song because things are going to appear that have something to do with the song.

Questions or Comments During a Song

The two following skits illustrate how a puppet can ask questions or make comments during pauses in a song. For this type of activity choose slow songs so a puppet can say his words without breaking the rhythm of the song. Or have the pianist and song leader hesitate each time the puppet speaks. Use this technique only on an occasional song—don't overdo it.

JESUS LOVES ME

CHILDREN:
(SINGING) Jesus loves me! This I know. . .
PUPPET:
How do you know?
CHILDREN:
For the Bible tells me so.
PUPPET:
Who belongs to Him?
CHILDREN:
Little ones to Him belong, They are weak but He is strong.
PUPPET:
Does Jesus love you?
CHILDREN:
(SING CHORUS)

DANIEL WAS A MAN OF PRAYER

(Tune: "Near the Cross," *Salvation Songs for Children* #3, page 44)

CHILDREN: Daniel was a man of prayer . . .
PUPPET: How do you know?
CHILDREN: Daily prayed he three times,
PUPPET: What happened then?
CHILDREN: Till one day they had him cast,
PUPPET: Where?
CHILDREN: In the den of lions.
PUPPET: What happened then?
CHILDREN: Even then, in the den, Fears could not alarm him . . .
PUPPET: Why?
CHILDREN: God just shut the lions' mouths, So they could not harm him.

Puppet Announces a Song

A puppet can announce the song that is to be sung, perhaps making a comment concerning the song.

BY GIVING CLUES
Instead of simply announcing the name of the song to be sung, a puppet can have children guess the name by giving clues in one of the following ways:

BY GIVING THE TUNE

Have a puppet 1) hum the first two notes of the song and then hum additional notes if needed, 2) hum a phrase within the song, or 3) hum the concluding notes starting with the *last* two notes and adding more if needed—the last three notes, the last four notes, etc.

BY GIVING A WORD OR WORDS

A puppet can say, or have on a sign card, a word or a phrase in the song.

BY USING AN OBJECT, PICTURE OR STICK DRAWING

An object, picture or stick drawing suggested by the song can appear in the stage or be in a box near the stage. The puppet would be in charge of having the item shown to the group. Or the item could be "fished" for. (Puppeteer places item on a spread-apart paper clip when pole is lowered into stage.) A candle would suggest "This Little Light of Mine"; an arrow, "One Way"; a smiling face, "Happiness Is the Lord"; a fish, "I Will Make You Fishers of Men."

BY ACTION

Have one or more puppets act out an event suggested by the song.

Puppet Learns a Song

A puppet can ask a group of boys and girls to teach him a song. The song could be one recently learned by the group or it could be a familiar song. Even if a puppet has heard the song before, or even sung it with the children, he can forget the words and have to learn it over again. A puppet might learn a song quickly sometimes and with difficulty other times.

CHILDREN TEACH A PUPPET

PUPPET: (ENTERS VOCALIZING) I just returned from my voice lesson. I learned a new song I'd like to teach to the boys and girls. (PUPPET SINGS A PORTION OF THE SONG OFF KEY OR USING SEVERAL IN-CORRECT WORDS, OR BOTH)
TEACHER: Whoa. . .I don't know who your voice teacher is, but I think the children could teach you that song better than your voice teacher did. (CHILDREN TEACH SONG TO PUPPET WHO EXPRESSES DELIGHT OVER LEARNING IT CORRECTLY)

TEACHER TEACHES A PUPPET

TEACHER: (STARTS TEACHING SONG TO CHILDREN)
PUPPET: Cut. . .cut. . .cut, please. That's too fast for me. How about going a little slower so I can learn the words.
TEACHER: (SAYS WORDS TO PUPPET, WAITING FOR PUPPET TO REPEAT EACH WORD OR PHRASE)
PUPPET: (REPEATS EACH WORD OR PHRASE IN A MONOTONE, GIVING EQUAL EMPHASIS TO EACH SYLLABLE)
TEACHER: Now sing with me.* (STARTS SINGING)
PUPPET: (SINGS WORDS IN A MONOTONE GIVING EQUAL EMPHASIS TO EACH SYLLABLE)
TEACHER: (STOPS PARTWAY THROUGH SONG) What's the matter?
PUPPET: You just taught me the words. How about teaching me the tune?
TEACHER: It goes like this. . .(SINGS SONG BY PHRASES, WAITING FOR PUPPET TO REPEAT EACH PHRASE)
PUPPET: Now I'm ready. Let's sing.**

*If the teacher is the puppeteer, ask the puppet to sing by himself.
**If the teacher is the puppeteer, the puppet asks to sing by himself. If you want the learning process repeated, have the puppet sing incorrectly and reteach the song by phrases.

Puppet Sings with Children

One or more puppets can just appear and sing with a group, or permission to sing along might be requested.
Children will enjoy alternating phrases, sentences or verses with a puppet.

PUPPET: Oh, who can make a flower? I'm sure I can't, can you?
CHILDREN: Oh, who can make a flower? No one but God 'tis true.

110

Puppet Leads a Song

BY VOICE

A puppet can lead a song simply by singing with a strong voice. If a group is divided, have one puppet in charge of each division. Or have a puppet and a person in charge of separate sides. A puppet might forget which side he's leading and sing at the wrong time.

PUPPET #1: I think the boys sang best.
PUPPET #2: I think the girls sang best.
PUPPET #1: Naw. . .the boys sang best.
PUPPET #2: The girls did.
PUPPET #1: Come to think of it, both the boys and the girls sang very well.
PUPPET #2: You're right. Let's sing again.

BY APPEARANCE

Sing when you see me. Instruct the group to sing only when they see the puppet. Have the puppet pop up and sing the first phrase or sentence of the song, having the children sing with him; then exit, pause, pop up, and sing the second phrase or sentence, having children sing with him. Continue to use this procedure throughout the song. The length of the pauses could vary. When the group has mastered this technique, have the puppet exit irregularly, sometimes in the midst of a phrase or sentence. During "people songs," the puppet should not sing but just appear as a cue for the children to sing.

Sing when you don't see me. Instruct the group to sing only when they don't see the puppet. Have the puppet sing the first phrase or sentence, then exit quickly. After the children have sung the second phrase or sentence, have the puppet pop up and sing the third phrase or sentence. When the group is used to this technique, have the puppet enter and exit irregularly.

BY ARM MOVEMENT

If a rod can be attached to the puppet's arm, he can lead singing with arm movements.

Puppet Teaches a Song

I FEEL LIKE SINGING

PUPPET #1: I feel so good I think I'll sing a song. (SINGS SONG NEW TO GROUP)
PUPPET #2: I feel so good I think I'll sing that song too. (IF THERE ARE TWO PUPPETEERS, BOTH PUPPETS SING)
TEACHER: I feel so good I think I'll sing with the puppet(s). Why don't you boys and girls join us?

SING IT RIGHT

PUPPET: Hi, kids, how about singing one of my favorite songs, (Name of song)?
TEACHER: I think the boys and girls would like to but they don't know that song.

111

PUPPET: Why don't you sing it for us so we can learn it? (PUPPET SINGS TOO FAST AND TOO LOUD) Sing it nicely! (PUPPET CLEARS THROAT, WITH MUCH ADO) Don't do that! (PUPPET CALMLY CLEARS THROAT) Now sing the song so the boys and girls can learn it.

PUPPET: O.K. (WHISPERS SONG)

TEACHER: You get one more chance. (PUPPET SINGS SONG AS IT SHOULD BE SUNG)

RAISE YOUR HAND IF I MAKE A MISTAKE*

PUPPET: I'm going to sing that song you just learned and I just might put in an extra word or leave a word out or change a word. You raise your hand if I make a mistake.

NOTE: Instead of raising a hand, children could clap their hands once. If two small groups are competing, each group could have a call bell to ring. (Call bells are available in stationery stores.)

*Mistakes may be humorous but be cautious of humor when the words concern a deep spiritual truth.

A DIFFICULT SONG TO LEARN

Hearing a song repeated and seeing a song visualized are both good methods of teaching a song. For example, in teaching "There Were Twelve Disciples," the teacher could place each disciple's name on the flannelboard or in a pocket chart as the puppet names it in the song. Or the teacher could have the names on display and point to each as it is named in the song. After the puppet has sung the song a few Sundays, have the class join in.

A "ROUND"

TEACHER: Boys and girls, today I have an exciting song for us to try. Pistachio has volunteered to help. (TURNING TO PISTACHIO) Now, Pistachio, the words are there on the chalkboard (or chart). Read them as I sing the song through once. (TEACHER STARTS SINGING—TO THE TUNE OF "ARE YOU SLEEPING?" PISTACHIO SAYS WORDS SPEEDILY IN A LOUD VOICE.)

> "Read your Bible, read your Bible,
> And you'll know how to grow
> To be more like Jesus
> To be more like Jesus
> Every day, read and pray."
> (Source of words unknown)

      Pistachio, I meant for you to read the words to yourself, silently, while I sing.

PISTACHIO: Sorry about that. I'll do it right this time.

TEACHER:	(SINGS. PISTACHIO READS SILENTLY. IF PISTACHIO FORGETS ONCE OR TWICE, TEACHER OR DESIGNATED CHILD MOMEN- TARILY HOLDS HIS MOUTH CLOSED.)
PISTACHIO:	Say, I like that song. (TO CHILDREN) You know, if you boys and girls read your Bible every day, you *will* grow to be more like Jesus.
TEACHER:	Let's all sing it together. (EVERYONE SINGS) Pistachio, do you know what a round is?
PISTACHIO:	Sure.
TEACHER:	Good! Would you please explain to the class?
PISTACHIO:	A round is. . .a circle?. . .Maybe I don't know what a round is.
TEACHER:	Could someone help us out? What is a round? (FROM DISCUSSION EXPLAIN THAT A ROUND IS A SONG IN WHICH DIFFERENT VOICES BEGIN SINGING THE SAME WORDS AT DIFFERENT TIMES) Understand, Pistachio?
PISTACHIO:	Right.
TEACHER:	Then let's demonstrate with our new song. I'll start, and after I've sung "Read your Bible, read your Bible,"you come in. O.K? Ready?
PISTACHIO:	Ready.

TEACHER AND PISTACHIO: (BOTH SINGING AT ONCE) Read your Bible, read. . .

TEACHER:	Stop! Wait! No, Pistachio, I sing first, then you sing. After I sing "Read your Bible" twice, you start. Ready now?
PISTACHIO:	Ready!
TEACHER:	(SINGING) Read your Bible, read your Bible, And you'll know how to. . . Pistachio!
PISTACHIO:	(NONCHALANTLY) Yes?
TEACHER:	You were supposed to sing. Boys and girls, maybe you'd better help Pistachio. Let's all try it. I'll start and you and Pistachio come in as I start the second line. O.K?

TEACHER, PISTACHIO AND CHILDREN: (ALL SING SONG AS IT SHOULD BE SUNG)

Puppet Emphasizes the Meaning of Words

QUESTIONS AND COMMENTS

The meaning of the words in a song can be emphasized by a listening puppet who asks questions or makes comments during pauses in a song (see QUESTIONS OR COMMENT DURING A SONG). Also question or comments before or after a song will place emphasis on the meaning of the words.

INTRODUCTION TO A SONG

PUPPET:	One of us puppets is supposed to sing a song today, but I don't know which one. Excuse me just a minute. . .I'll go down and see if I can find out who is going to sing and the name of the song. (EXITS, PAUSES, REENTERS) Well, the name of the song is (name of song). Now, if I could just find out who's supposed to sing. Excuse me again, please. (EXITS, PAUSES, REENTERS WITH ANOTHER PUPPET) Folks,

may I present (name of puppet) who is going to favor us by singing (name of song). (TO PUPPET #2) Say, how come you weren't up here on time?

PUPPET #2: Well, I got to thinking about the words in the song and forgot what I was supposed to be doing. Do you know who can make all those kids out there happy?*

PUPPET #1: As a matter of fact, yes, I do. . .it's Jesus, just like the song says. Ready. . . sing. . .

PUPPET #2: (SINGS THE SONG)

The question asked will depend on the song to be sung.

WRONG SONG

TEACHER: Roquefort, do you know a Sunday School song you could sing for us today?

ROQUEFORT: Sure.

TEACHER: Would you sing it for us right now?

ROQUEFORT: Sure. . .(SINGING) "I've been workin' on the railroad all the livelong day. I've. . ."

TEACHER: That's not a Sunday School song!

ROQUEFORT: Let me listen to myself. . ."I've been workin'. . ." How about that. . . you're right. I'm glad you pointed that out 'cause I'd much rather sing a Sunday School song. (TO CHILDREN) Boys and girls, you listen to the words as I sing and afterwards tell me why I'd rather sing a Sunday School song. Here goes. . .

CATCH MY MISTAKE

This idea is explained in the preceding section—for use with a song new to a group. Attention will be drawn to the meaning of words when children are asked to signal when a puppet sings a familiar song and substitutes one or more incorrect words.

THAT'S NOT HOW THAT SONG GOES

Song: "One Way"—published by National Child Evangelism Fellowship, West Coast Region.

PUPPET: (SINGING) Two ways God said to get to hea-ven.
I-I won-der what they are.
Three ways to reach those pearly mansions.
Wh-at ev-er could they be?
Yes, there are four. Yes, there are five. . .

TEACHER: (or another puppet): Hey, just a minute, that's not the way that song goes. It's supposed to be: "One way God said to get to heaven. Jesus is the only way." You listen as the boys and girls sing.

PUPPET: O.K., I'll listen very carefully. (LISTENS AS CHILDREN SING) But how do you know that Jesus is the only way to heaven?

TEACHER (or group): Because the Bible says so.

PUPPET: Then it's true. I think I can sing the words right now. (SINGS

CORRECTLY) (Or puppet might ask children to sing twice before he sings. If you wish to place even more emphasis on the words, have puppet say the words before he sings them.)

TYPES OF MIX-UPS. Mix-ups can involve doctrine, as in the sample script above. However, a mix-up can be simply changing one or more words—such as "get" to "fly" and "reach" to "teach"—with all other words sung correctly. If a puppet objects because an incorrect word has the same meaning as the correct one, insist that the puppet sing the words as written.

CAUTION. Be careful in choosing substitute words. Avoid words that might bring something undesirable into the minds of children.

DRAMATIZATION

Knowledge of how a song came to be written can make the words more meaningful. Bible bookstores have books on this subject. Puppets can dramatize incidents relating to the writing of a song.

MUSIC QUIZ

The following questions are examples of the types of questions for puppets to ask after a song period. Fun-type questions are interspersed to add interest.
1. What was the name of the first song we sang today?
2. Of all the songs we sang today, which song do you like best? Why?
3. Tell me the words in one of the songs that say who Jesus is.
4. What was the eleventh word of the first song?
5. How many letters (or "p's" or vowels) are in the word "happiness"?
6. Think of the second song we sang. Tell me what that song is saying in a sentence or two of your own.

Puppet Sings a Special Number

Puppets have a special fascination when they sing. A puppeteer need not have a good singing voice as most any voice coming from a puppet will be well received. A man, when singing for a child or woman, can sing falsetto or in a loud whisper.

On certain occasions you may wish to use a recorded song, with the puppet "mouthing" the words. If the voice on a record is a mature adult voice, try playing the record at a faster RPM than it was recorded. This will raise the level of the voice and give it a more puppet-like quality. The same technique can be used after recording a mature voice on a tape recorder with an RPM switch.

Unless the interest level of a song is unusually high, a puppet should not sing a long selection.

WHEN A PUPPET SINGS TO AN AUDIENCE

A puppet should not remain in one "frozen" position when singing but should sing to all parts of an audience. For action and added interest, a puppet might lean over the stage occasionally, and for ending notes point his nose in the air and quiver a bit.

For fun-type songs a puppet could turn his back to the audience and lean over the stage occasionally to sing a phrase or two. During interludes in a song a puppet with braids might sharply twist her head from side to side, in time to the music, so her braids will swing or the puppet could be swung in a circle. Also a puppet might scratch his neck, his ear or his tummy. A puppet could hold the last note of a song until an adult leader closes the puppet's mouth. On occasion a puppet might warm up: lah-lah-lah-lah; me-me-me-me; you-you-you-you; them-them-them-them.

You may wish to have a puppet normally sing a song correctly; but for variations a puppet could: (1) sing a song too fast; (2) sing parts of a song at the normal rate and a few phrases too slowly, while pausing to look around after each word; (3) sing parts of a song too loud and other parts too soft; (4) sing slightly off-key; (5) make up words to the correct tune or (6) sing the correct words to an original tune—perhaps singing up and down the scale, or singing one phrase on one note and succeeding phrases on different single notes. If a puppet does poorly, a teacher can: (a) comment that the puppet did his best, or must not be feeling well today, or (b) (either after or interrupting during the song) ask children for suggestions on how the puppet might want to change his behavior. Have the puppet receive all suggestions happily, heed the advice, and after the song ask the teacher if he did well.

TRY AGAIN

PUPPET #1:   (Name of puppet) is going to sing a selection today. I'm going to keep time for him as (WHISPERING) sometimes he has a bit of trouble. (NORMAL VOICE) Here he comes. (PUPPET #2 ENTERS) Are you ready?
PUPPET #2:   Ready.
PUPPET #1:   A-one, a-two. . .(PUPPET #1 WAVES ARM OR NODS HEAD IN CORRECT TIME. PUPPET #2 SINGS FIRST FEW NOTES CORRECTLY, THEN THE NEXT FEW NOTES TOO SLOWLY, THE NEXT FEW TOO FAST.) Stop. . .STOP. Let's start again. (PUPPET #2 SINGS CORRECTLY UNTIL MIDDLE OF SONG, THEN TOO SLOW AND TOO FAST AND IS STOPPED BY PUPPET #1) Let's try it again. . .from the beginning. (PUPPET #2 SINGS CORRECTLY UNTIL ALMOST THE END, THEN SPEEDS UP, TAKES A BOW IF POSSIBLE. EXITS) I give up! (PUPPET #1 FLOPS OVER STAGE IF

POSSIBLE, THEN STRAIGHTENS UP AND FAINTS BACKWARDS
OFF STAGE WITH A GROAN)

OFF-KEY SKIT

A puppet sings part of a song off-key. When this is brought to his attention by the teacher, another puppet or the children, he excuses himself, saying he is going to take a voice lesson. After the group sings a song or two, the puppet re-appears, comments on his voice lesson, and sings the song correctly or with only a slight problem. If he has a slight problem he announces that he'll practice and try again next week.

WHEN ONE PUPPET SINGS TO ANOTHER

A variety of movements can be used when one puppet sings to another. When Puppet #1 sings to Puppet #2, #2 can keep time to the music, keeping his eyes on #1 most of the time. Puppet #2 might look in #1's mouth once or twice when #1's mouth is wide open. Both puppets can sway a bit in time to the music, perhaps with heads together for brief periods and then they might sway in opposite directions. Puppet #1 might move closer to #2, with #2 backing up with each forward step of #1 until he's at the end of the stage. Puppet #1 could move to the center of the stage, and after a pause, #2 could move to the center of the stage. Both could then  keep time to the music together. Another action is for the puppets to move up and down in opposite order.

WHEN ONE PUPPETEER OPERATES TWO SINGING PUPPETS

If one puppeteer is working two singing puppets, have the puppets alternate phrases or sentences. To differentiate between voices, make one voice stronger or of a different quality, or have one puppet sing at a slower tempo than the other, or have one puppet sing an octave lower than the other.

Singing puppets should be held far enough apart to allow for movement right and left, except for times when their heads are together as for an occasional ending note. Use a variety of movements. Puppets can face each other, away from each other or in the same direction. Remember to have puppets sing to all parts of an audience. Puppets might also

117

walk a bit as they sing or during an interlude in the song.

CAUTION: A word of caution regarding movement to music is in order here. No movement should be of such a type as to be interpreted as dancing.

WHEN A PUPPET SINGS WITH A PERSON

If a puppet sings a duet with a person, make sure the words do not refer to a personal relationship with God. However, if just part of the words are appropriate for only a person to sing, the person could sing that part and the puppet sing or join in for the rest of the song.

BEFORE A SONG

Before a song is sung, puppets or a puppet and a person might talk about practicing, and clear their throats. They might disagree about what song they will sing or start singing different songs without disagreeing verbally before singing. They might start singing at different times and might fuss about who is going to sing. The fussing should be fun-type fussing and be followed by a happy solution.

The following two skits present ideas you may wish to use.

MAY I HELP?

RUFFORD: Hi, Shepley.
SHEPLEY: Hi, Rufford. (TO AUDIENCE) This is my friend, Rufford. (TO RUFFORD) I'm about to sing a song.
RUFFORD: What song?
SHEPLEY: (Name of song)
RUFFORD: Oh, I know that one. May I help you sing it?
SHEPLEY: That's a good idea. Ready. . .(THEY SING)

NO YOU'RE NOT, I AM

PUPPET #1:   (TO AUDIENCE) I'm going to sing (name of song).
PUPPET #2:   (ENTERING) No, I'm going to sing (name of song).
PUPPET #1:   No, no, no, I'm going to sing it.
PUPPET #2:   No you're not, I am.
PUPPET #1:   We have a problem.
PUPPET #2:   Yes, we do.* Do any of you boys and girls have a suggestion that would solve our problem?
CHILDREN: Take turns. . .both sing together. (IF THERE'S ONLY ONE PUP-PETEER, AND SING TOGETHER IS SUGGESTED, HAVE A PUPPET SAY, "There's only one person back there working us and she can't sound off with two voices at once so we'll have to think of something else." IF NECESSARY, A PUPPET SUGGESTS THEY EACH SING PART OF THE SONG AND ASK IF THAT WOULD WORK.)
PUPPET #1 AND #2:   (SING TOGETHER OR ALTERNATELY)

*If you do not wish audience participation continue the skit as follows:
PUPPET #1:   Let's not fuss. You can sing the song.
PUPPET #2:   (TO AUDIENCE) That makes me want to let him do it. (TO PUPPET #1) I know what. . .Let's both sing together (*Or both sing parts of the song*).
PUPPET #1 AND #2:   (SING TOGETHER OR ALTERNATELY)

118

THE "HUMMER"

The Hummer is a shy puppet (except on occasion). He never speaks; he only hums songs. Hummer closes his mouth when humming and opens his mouth to take breaths during pauses in a song.

COMFREY: Boys and girls, Hummer is with us today. Let's see if he can hum a song for us. (HUMMER WHISPERS IN COMFREY'S EAR) He says he'll try.

HUMMER: Hum-m-m-m-m (HUMS A FEW NOTES, THEN TURNS HIS HEAD INTO COMFREY'S SHOULDER, THEN WHISPERS IN COMFREY'S EAR)

COMFREY: Hummer says he wants you boys and girls to sing, "Jesus Loves the Little Children of the World," then maybe he could hum it. (CHILDREN SING)

HUMMER: (HUMS SONG*)

*On occasion, for a song in a lighter vein, Hummer might hum first quietly, then progressively more boldly, becoming very enthusiastic toward the end of the song.

SUGGESTION: Use Hummer only every five weeks or so with primaries; perhaps more often with pre-schoolers. If you don't have a separate puppet for Hummer, ask a regular puppet to hum or have a regular puppet ask to try to hum a song.

Puppet Includes a Song in a Skit

THERE IS SOMETHING YOU CAN DO is an example of a song used in a skit that involves a personal relationship with God on the part of at least one story character. Therefore, use only people puppets—do not use animal or monster-type puppets to represent Freddie and Stephany. Have puppets look mostly at each other—like a play on television.

THERE IS SOMETHING YOU CAN DO

Song	"There is Something You Can Do" Album "Marcy Sings to Children," Zondervan
Cast	Freddie (boy about four years old)
	Stephany (older girl)

FREDDIE: Hi, Stephany. I wish I were big so I could do things for Jesus like you can do.

STEPHANY: But Freddie, you can do something for Jesus.

FREDDIE: I can?

STEPHANY: Listen. . .(STEPHANY MOUTHS THE WORDS AS RECORD PLAYS

FIRST STANZA OF SONG. STEPHANY GLANCES ONLY OCCA-
SIONALLY AT AUDIENCE; LOOKS MOSTLY AT FREDDIE.
FREDDIE MAKES COMMENTS SUCH AS "REALLY!" AND "I
CAN?" DURING APPROPRIATE INTERLUDES IN SONG.) That's
right, Freddie. You can bring a friend to hear about Jesus.

FREDDIE: I'm going to do that.
STEPHANY: Do what?
FREDDIE: Bring a friend to hear about Jesus.
STEPHANY: O.K.
FREDDIE: I'll be right back. . .now don't go away. (FREDDIE EXITS. STEPHANY
SINGS SECOND STANZA. FREDDIE REENTERS WITH FRIEND
WHEN WORDS OF SONG INDICATE) Stephany, this is my friend,
Johnny. Will you tell him about Jesus?
STEPHANY: Yes I will, but you can help me.
FREDDIE: I can?
STEPHANY: Yes. . .let's go to my house for a snack and you can help me tell Johnny
about Jesus. (ALL EXIT)

How to Change a "People Song" to a "Puppet Song"

If a song is inappropriate for a friend puppet to sing, because the words imply a personal relationship to God, perhaps one or more words can be changed so the song is *declaring* truth rather than *applying* truth to the singer. In some cases, the substitute word(s) will need to be sung more quickly or more slowly than the original word(s) and a slight revision of the tune might be necessary.

For example: "I Love Him Better Every Day" can be changed to "You Should Love Him Better Every Day." "Wounded For Me" can be changed to "Wounded For You."

Or, another technique is to turn a statement into a question. For example: "I Have Decided to Follow Jesus" can be changed to "Have You Decided to Follow Jesus?"

NOTE: Make such changes only when a puppet sings to children—not when a puppet is singing with children. This is because word changes probably would not be heard when a puppet sings in combination with a group of children.

Using Animal Sounds Instead of Words

Animals can "sing," making the sound characteristic of their species instead of singing the words of a song. If a particular animal has no appropriate sound, invent one for him. Animals might accompany a person or another puppet who is singing the words. Animal sounds can be for "fun-type" songs, for the first verse of the birthday song or for the repetition of a welcome song. Animal puppets can participate during pauses in a song by making one or more sounds before the next word is sung by whoever is singing the song.

Dogs are versatile sound-makers because of the variety of their characteristic sounds—"arf-arf," "woof-woof," "ow-ow-ow." Even "bark-bark" can be used during a song. When one dog is singing, he might howl the whole song or sing "arf" on the higher notes and "woof" on the lower notes. When two dogs are singing, one might make one type of sound throughout and the other a different type, or both might sing the same sound for one phrase and a different sound for the next. When two or more dogs are singing, you may wish to have one howl only at the beginning of each phrase or sentence and hold the "o-o-o-o-o" sound throughout the phrase or sentence.

Children's Use of Puppets in Music

If you wish to involve children in puppetry, music is a good place to begin. Consider all the ways you plan to use puppets with music and ask yourself if a child, instead of an adult, could be the puppeteer. You may be surprised at what good puppeteers children make and how well they respond to being involved in puppetry.

A PUPPET FOR EACH YOUNG CHILD

One preschool department supplies each child with a small felt puppet for song time. All of the children are allowed to work their puppets at their seats as much as they wish (which is all the time!). The puppets "sing" to each other, to other children, and to the teachers.

A CHILD CAN LEAD A SONG WITH A PUPPET

After puppets have been introduced to a group, most young chidren will be anxious to work a puppet to lead a song in front of the class. You will probably want to let everyone have a turn, perhaps all on the same day if the group is small. Sometimes leading a song with a puppet could be a reward for good behavior, enthusiastic singing, or recitation of a memory verse. At other times you might choose the first leader and after the first song, have that child choose the next leader from those who indicate their desire to lead and have not yet participated. The number of leaders chosen would depend on the time allowed for singing.

PANTOMIME SINGING TO RECORDED MUSIC

Both young children and older children will enjoy the experience of using a puppet to pantomime singing to recorded music. For a more polished performance, have the puppeteer(s) practice ahead of time.

Children's Musical Presentations

Adding puppets to a children's choir presentation will result in increased interest of the children in the choir and also of the audience. The puppets might be worked by children or you could enlist the services of a youth or adult puppet team.

CHILDREN'S
CHOIR

WHAT PUPPETS CAN DO

Puppets can introduce songs, sing with children, sing parts of a song alternately with children, sing solo or small group parts, and perform speaking and acting parts. If a children's choir is presenting a musical that has been recorded, puppets can perform the speaking and solo or small group singing parts while pantomiming the words to the recording. The children's choir can perform the group singing parts with live accompaniment—not using the recording.

CARE IN SELECTION OF SONGS

Take care in the selection of songs for puppets to sing so that puppets that are not "story puppets" do not sing "people songs." If the words children sing set the scene for a dramatic performance, then puppets can be considered "story puppets" and sing and speak the solo and small group speaking and singing parts and perform the story action. An example of this type of musical is "Cool in the Furnace," written by Buryl Red and Grace Hawthorne (Word Records WST 8580). A strip of red cellophane raised in front of the puppets during the furnace scene is effective.

In a musical, if "story puppets" represent people who have a relationship to God, then these puppets should not sing in combination with children. Puppets that sing *with* children are "friend puppets" and friend puppets should not pretend to be capable of a relationship with God.

STAGES

If a puppet is used for the Master of Ceremonies, you may wish to have a separate stage for him. If an open stage (stage at left) is used, backgrounds descriptive of songs can be hung from a framework of plastic pipe or attached to a portable chalkboard or bulletin board. Backgrounds can be pulled off, or otherwise changed for the next song. If an enclosed stage (stage at right) is used, props suggested by a song could appear in the opening with the puppet(s).

10
Puppets Use Musical Instruments

With some practice and dexterity puppets can be made to use certain musical instruments with surprising success.

RHYTHM INSTRUMENTS

Puppets can accompany group singing using rhythm instruments such as Christmas jingle bells or a triangle. A toy that squeaks when squeezed or a bicycle horn could also be used for this purpose. Have a puppet play an instrument during the singing or keep time during interludes in a song. The sound from a bicycle horn can be muffled by taping a

piece of crumpled paper toweling in the horn. A triangle or bicycle horn can be attached to a stage or held in position by a person outside the stage. A puppet may need a rod-controlled arm for bells or a triangle.

KAZOO

A kazoo is probably the easiest instrument for one puppeteer to handle for the playing of a tune as a tune need merely be hummed into the instrument, and a kazoo requires only one of a puppeteer's hands. No hands are required if a kazoo is attached to a harmonica holder as indicated below. Kazoos are available in toy and music stores. A metal kazoo makes a better sound than a plastic one.

KAZOO FOR PUPPET

When a puppet is on stage and needs a kazoo, the puppet can excuse himself, exit, and reenter after taking the kazoo in his mouth from the hand of the puppeteer or from a TV tray or holder in the stage. A kazoo could be placed outside the stage and a puppet request a child to place it in his mouth. When finished with the kazoo a puppet can exit, release the kazoo, and reenter with his mouth free for speech.

If a puppet speaks with a kazoo in his mouth, the speech should be somewhat muffled.

If a kazoo easily slips out of a puppet's mouth, use contact cement to glue a strip of foam or felt around the kazoo near the mouth end—to form a "bump" for the puppet to grasp. More than one layer of foam or felt may be needed.

If a puppet has a rod-controlled arm and the puppeteer has a hand available to hold the rod, wire a kazoo to the puppet's hand using chenille wires or pipe cleaners.

KAZOO FOR PUPPETEER

Of course the puppet cannot bring forth any sounds from a kazoo. The puppeteer must do this. A puppeteer working one puppet can hold a kazoo in his free hand and place it to his mouth when needed. If both hands are holding puppets, the kazoo can be taped to a harmonica holder. Holders are inexpensive and available in music stores. A holder enables a puppeteer to talk and also to play the kazoo whenever he wishes. Wrap cloth tape (Mystik or duct tape) around a kazoo near the mouth end so a puppeteer's teeth can grasp the kazoo firmly.

For certain occasions you may wish to add a squeak toy like a plastic ear of corn and/or a bicycle horn to a harmonica holder. They would be operated by the bite of the puppeteer's teeth. A bicycle horn or squeak toy can also be placed on the floor and operated with the pressure of a puppeteer's foot.

When a puppeteer plays a kazoo for a puppet, the puppeteer should be behind a stage so he cannot be seen by the audience.

YELPER PLAYS THE KAZOO

TEACHER: Did you know that Yelper can play the kazoo? (YELPER NODS HIS HEAD) Go get your kazoo, Yelper, and play for the boys and girls. (YELPER EXITS, REENTERS WITH KAZOO) O.K., How about a tune? (YELPER NODS HEAD, "YES," AND PLAYS ONE SHORT NOTE) Well, now you're warmed up. . .let's have the tune. (YELPER FACES TEACHER, AUDIENCE, RIGHT, LEFT, TURNS HEAD UPSIDE DOWN AND PLAYS A SHORT UNRELATED NOTE WITH EACH CHANGE IN POSITION) Yelper, that's not much of a song! (YELPER PLAYS THREE NOTES OF "ONLY A BOY NAMED DAVID") What's the matter?. . .Did you forget the song? (YELPER NODS HEAD) Well, I guess you'll have to do it another day. (YELPER LOOKS AT AUDIENCE . . .TEACHER. . .BACK TO AUDIENCE AND PLAYS SONG WITH SOME PHRASES TOO FAST, SOME TOO SLOW, SOME AT NORMAL TEMPO BUT WITH HEAD IN DIFFERENT POSITIONS INCLUDING NOSE IN AIR AND HEAD REVOLVING IN A CIRCLE WHILE SLURRING ENDING NOTE.* YELPER PLAYS ENDING TOO FAST, DROPS KAZOO BEHIND STAGE, FACES AUDIENCE AND PANTS.)

*TO SLUR A NOTE: hum the correct note, then slide your voice either up or down the scale (few notes or several notes up or down), then slide your voice back to the original note. You will probably want to do this only once or twice during the song.

NOTE: If you wish the song played correctly, tell Yelper he'll be allowed to accompany the group as they sing the next song if he plays well, which he does, both for his special number and for the group singing.

GUESS THE SONG

PART I

PUPPET #1: I've been practicing a lot and I'm really quite good.

PUPPET #2: Quite good at doing what?

PUPPET #1: At playing the kazoo.

PUPPET #2: You're kidding!

PUPPET #1: No, I'm not. . .you want to hear me play?

PUPPET #2: I'm not sure. What song would you play?

PUPPET #1: You have to guess.

PUPPET #2: I'm not good at guessing, but I have a feeling these boys and girls are good guessers.

PUPPET #1: O.K., I'll play the beginning of the song and they can guess what song it is.

PUPPET #2: O.K.

PUPPET #1: I'll go get my kazoo. (EXITS, RETURNS WITH KAZOO AND PLAYS ONE NOTE) (Or kazoo can be outside the stage and the puppet ask a child to place the kazoo in his mouth.)

PUPPET #2: One note! All songs start with one note! You'll have to play more than one note.

PUPPET #1: (PLAYS FIRST TWO NOTES)

PUPPET #2: Can anyone guess this song? (PLAY AS MANY NOTES AS NECESSARY UNTIL SONG IS GUESSED) They guessed the song. Now are you going to play it?

PUPPET #1: (SHAKES HEAD, "NO")

PUPPET #2: Why not?

PUPPET #1: (HUMS IN KAZOO AS IF SAYING) I want the boys and girls to sing while I play.

PUPPET #2: You want the boys and girls to sing while you play?

PUPPET #1: (NODS HEAD, "YES")

PUPPET #2: Boys and girls, will you sing while he plays? (GROUP SINGS AS PUPPET PLAYS)

PART II

PUPPET #1: (ENTERS WITH NO KAZOO) Hi, (OPENS MOUTH AND KAZOO IS HEARD) how are you today?

PUPPET #2: Did you make a kazoo noise?

PUPPET #1: Yep. (OPENS MOUTH AS NOISE IS HEARD)

PUPPET #2: How can you make a kazoo noise without a kazoo?

PUPPET #1: Well. . .it's this way. . .I was playing with my kazoo awhile ago and I guess I swallowed it! (OPENS MOUTH AS KAZOO IS HEARD)

PUPPET #2: Will it play when you want it to?

PUPPET #1: I think so. (OPENS MOUTH AS KAZOO IS HEARD)

PUPPET #2: Do you want the boys and girls to guess a couple of songs today?

PUPPET #1: Sure, why (KAZOO NOISE) . . .oops, I mean why not? (SONGS ARE GUESSED AND SUNG)

PART III

PUPPET #1: (ENTERS WITH KAZOO)
PUPPET #2: What are you doing with a kazoo? I thought you swallowed one and it played whenever you wanted it to.
PUPPET #1: (HUMS ON KAZOO AS IF TO SAY) I can't get it to play anymore.
PUPPET #2: You can't get the one you swallowed to play anymore? (#1 SHAKES HEAD, "NO") But now you have a new one. (#1 NODS HEAD, "YES") Well, now we're back to normal. How about playing a couple of notes so we can guess the song.

GUITAR AND TRUMPET

A puppet with arms that can be controlled by a rod can "play" a guitar or a trumpet to a recording or actual instrument which is hidden from view. To make a puppet-size guitar: cut a guitar shape from wood paneling or cardboard. Glue two shapes together if extra stiffness is needed and reinforce the neck area of the guitar. Paint flowers or other design on the guitar if desired. Attach a neck strap (ribbon or fancy trim) to the guitar by poking chenille wires or pipe cleaners through holes made in the ends of the strap and in the guitar. Attach the left arm of the puppet to the guitar and control the right hand with a rod. When the puppet will be singing while playing, it will be helpful to have a second person control the puppet's right hand.

A toy trumpet can be wired to both hands of a puppet and the hands controlled by a rod. Move the trumpet away from the puppet's mouth and have the puppet "breathe" during interludes in the music.

126

RESOURCE LIST

PUPPETRY BOOKS

(If books are not available from your bookstore, write to the publisher for mail order information.)

A VARIETY BOOK OF SCRIPTS, Sarah Walton Miller. Broadman Press, 127 Ninth Avenue North, Nashville, TN 37234. Scripts for children, youth, and adults.

BIBLE PUPPET SCRIPTS, Diane Warner. Accent Books, P.O. Box 15337, Denver, CO 80215. 24 short Bible and contemporary scripts on 12 different themes. A puppet tells the story to 1 or 2 other puppets who interact with the storyteller.

GENESIS COMES TO LIFE!, Bea Carlton. Accent Publications, P.O. Box 15337, Denver, CO 80215.

PUPPET ANIMALS TELL BIBLE STORIES, Marie Chapman. Accent Books, P.O. Box 15337, Denver, CO 80215. Bible stories for younger children, each told by an animal that might have seen it happen. Patterns and instructions for making the puppets from oatmeal box, paper bags, and cloth.

PUPPET DIALOGUES, Charles E. Magnet. Accent Books, P.O. Box 15337, Denver CO 80215. 24 short Bible story scripts. A puppet tells the story to 1 or 2 other puppets who interact with the storyteller.

PUPPETS HELP TEACH, Diane Warner. Accent Books, P.O. Box 15337, Denver, CO 80215. 25 short Bible stories, Christian living stories, special occasion, and holiday scripts for younger children.

THE PUPPET AND THE WORD, Rolan Sylwester. Concordia Publishing House, 3558 S. Jefferson Ave., St. Louis, MO 53118. Patterns and directions for making puppets, scripts, ideas.

PUPPET PATTERNS AND READY-MADE PUPPETS

BACKES PATTERNS, P.O. Box 582, South Saint Paul, MN 55075. Basic patterns that can make 12 different animals. $5.50 postpaid.

LOCAL TOY STORES, RUMMAGE SALES, and GOODWILL STORE OUTLETS. Look for puppets that have good eye contact with an audience.

OUR FATHER'S PUPPET KINGDOM, P.O. Box 384, Ridgecrest, NC 28770. Soft sculpture, standard, and made-to-order puppets. Write for information.

PRINCE PUPPETS, 4819 King Road, Allison Park, PA 15101. Standard and made-to-order puppets. Write for information.

SHERAM PUPPETS, 61 West Lawn Avenue, Columbus, OH 43207. Large variety of puppets. Write for information.

SOCK PUPPETS BY MISS MELBA. Melba Connally, 16693 Evergreen Circle, Fountain Valley, CA 92708. Book of sock puppet instructions. $5.50 postpaid.

OTHER SOURCES OF PUPPETRY SUPPLIES

HIGLEY PUBLISHING CORP., P.O. Box 2470, Jacksonville, FL 32202. 136 Bible, Christian Living and Missionary puppet scripts. Write for brochure.

PUPPET PALS CO., 100 Belhaven Dr., Los Gatos, CA 95032. Puppet patterns, ready-made puppets, scripts, books, tapes, etc. Write to Dept. A for brochure.

THE PUPPETRY STORE, 1525 S.E. 24th St., Auburn, WA 98002. This is the Puppeteers of America bookstore. They carry many secular and some Christian puppetry books. For information send a self-addressed, stamped envelope (approximately 9" x 4" size). Envelope not required, but helpful.

ORGANIZATIONS AND PUBLICATIONS

CHILDREN'S BIBLE HOUR, Box 1, Grand Rapids, MI 49501. Send $5.00 donation for year subscription to *Cheery Chats and Challenges*—each issue includes a script. They also publish *Keys For Kids*— each booklet has about 60 stories that can be adapted for puppets. Write for a free copy of *Keys For Kids*.

FELLOWSHIP OF CHRISTIAN PUPPETEERS, F.C.P. Mail Center, P.O. Box 4361, Englewood, CO 80155. They sponsor conventions and publish a newsletter. Write for information.

FELLOWSHIP OF CHRISTIAN MAGICIANS, P.O. Box 1027, Wheaton, IL 60189. Their annual convention includes workshops on puppetry and ventriloquism. They also publish a quarterly newsletter. Write for information.

PUPPETEERS OF AMERICA, c/o Gail Schluter, #5 Cricklewood Path, Pasadena, CA 91107. A secular organization that sponsors monthly area meetings, and regional and national conventions that are helpful to the beginner and the advanced puppeteer. Their magazine is geared mostly for the advanced puppeteer. Write for information.